Venezuela in the Wake of Radical Reform

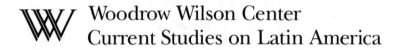

Woodrow Wilson Center
Current Studies on Latin America

Published with the Latin American Program
of the Woodrow Wilson International Center for Scholars
Joseph S. Tulchin, Director

Venezuela in the Wake of Radical Reform

edited by
Joseph S. Tulchin
with Gary Bland

Lynne Rienner Publishers • Boulder & London

Published in the United States of America in 1993 by
Lynne Rienner Publishers, Inc.
1800 30th Street, Boulder, Colorado 80301

and in the United Kingdom by
Lynne Rienner Publishers, Inc.
3 Henrietta Street, Covent Garden, London WC2E 8LU

Library of Congress Cataloging-in-Publication Data
Venezuela in the wake of radical reform / edited by Joseph S. Tulchin
   with Gary Bland
   (Woodrow Wilson Center current studies on Latin America)
   Includes bibliographical references and index.
   ISBN 1-55587-364-2 (pbk. : alk. paper)
   1. Venezuela—Politics and government—1974- .
2. Pérez, Carlos Andréz. 3. Venezuela—Economic policy.
4. Venezuela—Foreign relations. I. Tulchin, Joseph S., 1939- .
II. Bland, Gary. III. Series.
F2328.V47 1993
987.063'3—dc20   92-33571
                                          CIP

British Cataloguing in Publication Data
A Cataloguing in Publication record for this book
is available from the British Library.

Printed and bound in the United States of America

The paper used in this publication meets the requirements
of the American National Standard for Permanence of
Paper for Printed Library Materials Z39.48-1984.

Contents

CONTENTS

Preface

Joseph S. Tulchin

It is ironic that one of the Latin American Program's objectives in convening a conference on Venezuela in 1990 was to focus attention in the United States on a country that, because of its stability, seemed to lack, for scholars and policymakers alike, the attraction of the civil wars or revolutionary upheaval that drew attention to other parts of the region. We believed that the ambitious path of economic restructuring on which Venezuela had embarked, together with the reform of the state that was being proposed, deserved serious consideration. We believed the very stability of the system deserved our attention, and our respect. Today, of course, there is no difficulty finding renewed interest in Venezuela. As we move to publish this volume that emerged from the conference in 1990, we remain startled by the two coup attempts—in February and November—to oust President Carlos Andrés Pérez. Although both attempts failed, 1992 clearly has been a rough year for the Venezuelan president and the country's 34-year-old democracy.

Obviously, tremendous difficulties are inherent in the radical economic and political adjustment that is still underway throughout Latin America, as well as in other areas of the world. While many might argue that such dramatic change is long overdue and essential for countries whose economies faced collapse, mistakes, problems in implementation, and the unanticipated social consequences of striving for these goals in such rapid fashion can easily rattle a fragile democracy to its core. Venezuela is a stunning example.

The link between Pérez's radical reform program and his current troubles is unmistakable. Yet, it is not a sufficient explanation of the crisis facing the country today. Venezuela's unique historical development, the role of oil, and the strength of the political parties are among the essential considerations as well. These are the issues we address in this volume, focusing on the motivations behind the political and economic reform program and its impact on the Venezuelan economic and political system. We hope this book will provide food for thought for those in Latin America and elsewhere facing similar challenges and difficulties.

A great deal of effort and dedication went into the production of this volume. Andrés Stambouli first conceived the idea, lined up the Venezuelan participants, and then contributed important time, effort, and support to ensure that the conference and this volume were successful. Moisés Naím, who moved to Washington, D.C., shortly after the conference and who provided both the central chapter on economic reform and an epilogue, was an important source of inspiration in the effort to bring the project to fruition. I also want to thank all of our Venezuelan friends who traveled to the Wilson Center to participate in the conference.

I extend my deep appreciation to the staff of the Latin American Program for their work in this effort. Gary Bland, our senior program associate, guided the manuscript through the publication process, providing his writing and editing skills throughout. Lucy Hetrick, our program assistant, provided valuable assistance with the conference preparations. Finally, copy editor Leah Florence was again counted on to sharpen the text and to convert conference transcriptions into publishable form.

Joseph S. Tulchin

Introduction

Carlos Guerón

The characteristic features of the Venezuelan political system during the first three decades of the present democratic period are well known to scholars and students of the country, Venezuelans and North Americans alike.

The state controls the wealth produced by petroleum and is therefore the principal distributor of the surpluses generated by oil in a regulated and subsidized economy. The political system is built on a pact among members of the elites, under which the dominant political parties are the principal actors. The parties are much more than vehicles for the expression of the popular will. Through a vast array of clientelistic networks, they have become components of the social pressure on the state, while they also manipulate these pressures directly. The parties organized civic structures, dominated recruiting mechanisms, and provided the system with its ideological legitimacy. The predominant political culture gave the state, controlled by the parties, the roles of principal owner of the country's natural resources, leading investor, and main creator of employment by which it could generate demand for consumer goods. Consumer goods were produced by a private industrial sector developed through import substitution, which had become dependent on subsidies, overprotected, inefficient, and noncompetitive, operating under monopolistic or quasi-monopolistic conditions.

The state operates mines, produces raw materials and energy—petroleum, gas, petrochemicals, bauxite, iron, alumina, aluminum, steel, and semimanufactured goods—and is involved in banking, shipping, and other commercial services, sea and air transport, construction, education, health care, and public sanitation. It provides newsprint, owns the communication system's wavelengths, leases frequencies to radio and TV stations, oversees the telephone network, and generates, transmits, and distributes electricity, gas, and water. In addition, the state regulates and controls every phase of private productive activity: It grants licenses, fixes prices of materials,

Carlos Guerón is graduate professor of international relations and negotiations at the School of International Studies and International Economy at the Central University of Venezuela, Caracas.

1

regulates salaries, sets the cost of money by controlling interest rates; it finances, guarantees, and authorizes subsidies, protects the market by tariffs or import restrictions, sets consumer prices, decides tax rates, allows exemptions, collects its obligations, and condones debts.

The organized political parties not only compete for control of the state, but can also define the institutional life of trade and labor unions, universities, professional organizations, and producers' associations. They even dominate the elections of the governing boards of vacation clubs through their influence over the election of officials. The party elections held every five years are truly popular festivals, with bingo, sweepstakes, orchestras, singing, and dancing—enormous meetings attended by thousands of potential voters from the neighborhood and surrounding areas. Voters are transported in buses flying flags with each party's colors: white for the Acción Democrática (AD), green for the Social Christian party (COPEI), and yellow for the Democratic Republican Union (URD).

The electoral system, based on the Hondt system, operates with lists of candidates selected by the parties themselves, thus assuring proportional representation for minorities and stimulating the proliferation of party slates. Elections have been held with as many as seventeen candidates for president. Although these norms favored a multiparty system, the voting of the electorate progressively produced basically a two-party regime that gives a quasi-monopoly to the AD and COPEI.

Both the AD and COPEI parties, affiliated respectively with the International Social Democrats and the International Christian Democrats, adopted a Leninist model of centralized organization based on dividing the country regionally into manageable bureaus of professionals, youths, women, workers, farmers, and so forth. Party discipline has been rigid. Central authorities designated candidates for local offices and even to offices in organizations under the jurisdiction of committees of the legislative bodies. They named judges and officers of government-controlled unions, professional organizations, and universities. Disciplinary committees severely punished perceived deviations from or contradictions to the party line.

The unquestionable authority of the leaders, who usually belonged to the generation of the parties' founders, gave them almost limitless power. Their authority was reinforced by their legendary deeds in the struggle against the dictatorship and their roles as caudillos with widespread popularity among the masses. For decades, figures a little larger than life such as Rómulo Betancourt, Rafael Caldera, and Jóvito Villalba dominated public life and the parties they all but monopolized.

In the decade of the 1970s the traditional political and economic system reached its peak of success. The surplus income provided by the oil boom resulted from increases in prices (in US$) that began at a little over $2 a barrel, then jumped to $12, then to $14, and then reached the dizzying heights of $20, $30, and at one point almost $40 a barrel. Despite the halfhearted attempt to withhold part of the funds to lessen their impact on an economy unprepared to absorb this enormous mass of money, the surge of cash soon became an avalanche.

This buildup of wealth occurred toward the end of President Rafael Caldera's term in office (1969–1974), but its full impact was not felt until the presidency of Carlos Andrés Pérez (1974–1979). Venezuela then felt the results of the nationalization of the country's petroleum and iron and of the attempts to build a Great Venezuela based on gigantic public investments and massive increases in the size of the state, public expenditures, public employment, subsidies, and imports. The state became deeply indebted to the international banking system in financing both these investment programs and the payrolls of state institutions that had acquired the autonomy to borrow abroad unbeknownst to the central government. All of this provoked an accelerated growth of a middle class that consumed imports and began to travel, flooding the shops of Miami with their petrodollars, repeating the refrain: "It's so cheap that I'll take two." Consumerism, indebtedness, fixed interest costs that were below the rate of inflation, fixed exchange rates, free convertibility, tax exemptions, and easy, inexpensive credit, often accepted with no intention of repaying it, all characterized this period.

In such a context, this windfall, instead of being managed with common sense—for example taking into account an eventual fall in oil prices as was timidly suggested by the more skeptical—was poorly administered. Given the expenditures of the state, in spite of the waste, imports of luxury goods, investments in public projects that were often left unfinished, indiscriminate subsidies, unrecoverable loans, and the foreign debt, there was economic growth. But corruption made its appearance. There was dramatic growth in the state bureaucracy. The government issued decrees that obliged businesses to generate unproductive jobs—elevator operators, for example, and attendants for bathrooms used by the general public—and "salary subsidies" to grant income to people who neither studied nor worked.

Populism, patronage, and arbitrary and unequal distribution all fed on what was called the piñata of the public till. Venezuela received more money following the oil boom of the 1970s than it had received cumulatively throughout its entire previous history. Animated by Venezuela's new role in OPEC, the country's leaders asserted for their country a new, more influential role in the international community. They called for a new international economic system based on the protection of raw material prices, access to markets in industrialized nations for traditional and nontraditional exports from the developing world, transfer of capital and technology to underindustrialized countries, elimination of Cold

War bipolarity in great-power treatment of underdeveloped countries, and reduction of military expenditures by developed nations in order to make more resources available to assist the poorer countries of the world. To implement this new world order, they sponsored the creation of the Economic System for Latin America (SELA) and offered to house it in Caracas.

Some argued that OPEC was unique, while others said that it represented the beginning of a new era of cartelization by raw material producers that would change the structure of global economic power. Neomercantilists and liberals debated how the United States would face the double challenge presented by OPEC and the increasing competitiveness of Japan and Europe. But within a decade the large sums of money transferred to OPEC as a result of the rise in oil prices returned to the industrial centers as payment for massive imports of arms, machinery, consumer goods, and an ever-growing debt. Thus the terms of the debate in the international system, which appeared so favorable to the developing countries that exported primary products, changed again in the 1980s.

Besides the OPEC countries that had benefited from the boom in oil prices and Israel, Turkey, and Egypt, which were the principal beneficiaries of economic and military aid from the government of the United States, non-OPEC oil exporters like Mexico were the first countries to suffer the consequences of the "debt time-bomb." Due dates for the massive payment of interest and capital began to mature in the initial years of the 1980s. The international financial system, including the large US banks menaced by massive defaults from large debtors like Mexico, Argentina, Brazil, and to a lesser degree, Venezuela, appeared panic-stricken.

Venezuela reacted slowly to the situation. The government of Luis Herrera Campins (1979–1984) tried unsuccessfully to obtain credit from Japan in order to consolidate all of the country's overdue and pending interest and principal payments. And although there was still another increase in the price of oil in 1980, the imminence of the crisis, the loss of international credit because of the cessation of payments, and the erratic economic policy of the government produced a massive flight of capital that left the economy stagnant. The bolivar was devalued for the first time in twenty years, but the effects of the devaluation were vitiated by subsidies to so-called essential imports. Interest rates were held below the rate of inflation, the problem of refinancing the debt was delayed every ninety days, savings continued to flee abroad, and the first signs of the delegitimization of the party patronage system began to be seen. Municipal elections, for the first time scheduled to occur on a date different from the presidential election, produced unprecedented absenteeism in a country that until then had been characterized by a high degree of voter participation in elections. Venezuelans began to accuse the two-party system and the electoral system itself of causing the crisis.

The return to power of AD and the election of Jaime Lusinchi to the presidency (1984–1989) marked the beginning of the end. Determined to salvage the remains of the populist system, which had fallen into crisis, the government succeeded in implementing a totally unrealistic plan for restructuring the foreign debt, dedicating over half of the income from oil exports to debt repayment, maintaining differential exchange rates for financing imports, and, due to the lack of sufficient foreign exchange, authorizing letters of credit in subsidized—and in reality nonexistent— dollars, by which the government guarantees private foreign debt for real or imaginary imports. These errors further encouraged corruption and rapidly accelerated the dissipation of the remaining foreign exchange reserves.

The marital and extramarital affairs of the president (a ferocious divorce suit and a flagrant affair between the president and his private secretary, upon whom he had bestowed extraordinary political and economic power to administer public favors, contracts, and the granting of preferential dollars) emerged simultaneously with serious problems concerning the financing of state expenditures, the drying up of private investment, and capital flight. Inflation, devaluation, the depletion of foreign reserves, the loss of credibility of the political system and its elite, and the declining ability of the political parties to articulate and satisfy social demands added to the crisis.

Holding a mere $300 million in international operating reserves, the government was confronted with a grim situation in 1989. Faced with the requirement to pay more than $5 billion per year on its external debt, which represented more than half of the total income in foreign exchange from exports, unable to access international credit, hobbled by a balance-of-payments deficit, and carrying a fiscal deficit equal to almost 9 percent of the GNP, the government dramatically shifted its approach. It had become clear that as long as it persisted in maintaining a monetary system with multiple exchange rates (which encouraged excessive imports) keeping interest rates below the rate of inflation (which discouraged savings and investment and stimulated the constant decapitalization of the country) and preserving duties and unrealistically subsidized prices, the government had to struggle through crises with no capacity to assure adequate distribution of goods and services and a more equitable distribution of wealth. The system for the most part had insured indirect subsidies to the producer and stimulated the clandestine export of subsidized goods originally produced for domestic consumption at prices far below their international value. This process created shortages that primarily hurt those Venezuelans with the least resources— the very citizens for whom the subsidies had been designed in the first place—and set back the incorporation of new technology that could have made the production system more efficient and competitive. Thus it was that, as the Lusinchi administration came to an end, a critical economic, social, and political situation was coming to a head.

The Adjustment and the Sharp Change in Direction

The situation required a simultaneous attack on two fronts. A package of immediate adjustments designed (1) to reestablish the country's macroeconomic balance and permit renewed access to international financing, and (2) a medium- and long-term policy to radically reorient the Venezuelan economy. At the same time, it was necessary to reorganize the state and its basic institutions. This is the herculean task that confronted Carlos Andrés Pérez—as he was fully aware—when he returned to the presidency in 1989. The new president acted immediately.

What was under consideration in 1989 was the switch from a planned economy to an economy predominantly based on free market principles. The plan was to use the regulatory and supervisory power of the state to set the foundation for a less-controlled economy; to use the state's enormous petroleum resources to provide incentives for the generation of wealth through private enterprise; and to transform the system of protectionism, patronage, and subsidized aid inherently tied to the official budget into a system open to local and international competition. Moreover, the aim was to consolidate a transparent pricing structure set by market conditions, complement state investment with private investment in basic infrastructure, and promote increased productivity in the private sector. All of this had to be done without sacrificing the state's responsibility for the citizen's health and education, its duty to protect the most vulnerable economic and social sectors of the population, and its obligation to social security and environmental preservation. All of this was to be accomplished in a country in which the state and its expenditures are inevitably essential because the state owns the primary source of wealth: oil. It also owns the basic industries of iron, steel, aluminum, and electricity.

To initiate this process of transformation it was necessary to rectify immediately the imbalances in the fiscal, monetary, foreign exchange, commercial, and financial sectors. Inflation had to be cut and the differentials in the foreign exchange market had to be eliminated in order to achieve an exchange parity that would reflect the international position of the country's economy. Subsidies had to be removed. Additional required steps were: elimination of the fiscal deficit by reducing expenditures, increasing income, adjusting prices and duties for public services and goods; closing the gap in the balance of payments; reducing

the debt burden and refinancing it on terms compatible w
country's growth rate; returning to the international credit
reversing the flow of capital by encouraging domestic investments; and
attracting local and international private capital.

Upon restoring macroeconomic balance, the Pérez government
would initiate the transformation to an open economy oriented toward
exports and based on efficiency, competition, and the country's competitive and comparative advantages. Pérez would diversify production,
exports, and foreign markets by privatizing state companies; reconvert
state and private industries to make them efficient and competitive; and
implement a commercial policy to create incentives for competition and
increased competence. Laws regulating investment to eliminate differences in the treatment of local and foreign capital; limitations on
regulations so as to allow increased investment, reinvestment, and the
repatriation of funds abroad; and the free disposition of earnings were
seen as imperative. Pérez also planned to introduce a modern, flexible
tax system that would simultaneously reduce the fiscal dependency on
oil income, create incentives for reinvestment and employment, and
distribute the tax burden more evenly through the implementation of a
value-added tax.

The first phase of the adjustment program was a success, but it
exacted a high sociopolitical cost. Once the exchange rate differentials
and most of the subsidies were eliminated, interest rates rose, discour-
aging private investment. The debt was refinanced with an imaginative
menu of options: immediate payments with discounts, bonds with dis-
counted capital, reduced interest charges, and interest pegged to the
price of oil. Programs for converting debt into investment, guarantees
on debt principal through use of zero-coupon bonds issued by the US
Treasury, and, finally, instruments with interest payments deferred for
up to fourteen months were elements of the debt alleviation plan. All of
this was financed by loans from the International Monetary Fund (IMF)
and the World Bank. Both institutions, in addition, helped to rebuild the
country's international reserves and supported investment programs for
improving social infrastructure and increasing productivity.

On February 27, 1989, soon after the announcement of the adjustment program, which produced higher prices for public transport and
gasoline, Venezuela witnessed a massive series of public demonstrations
and riots leading to the loss of hundreds of lives. During the first year of
the adjustment program, the rate of inflation reached 80 percent,
unemployment climbed to 10 percent, private investment came to a
standstill, and interest rates rose 40 percent. But the macroeconomic
policies produced results in a much shorter time than even the most
optimistic observers expected: the fiscal deficit fell from 9 percent to 1
percent of the GNP, exports rose, the balance of payments deficit almost

disappeared; the bolivar was stabilized without exchange controls, capital returned to the country, international credit reappeared, and public sector investments in social infrastructure or in projects to stimulate production began. Domestic investments in the petroleum sector augmented its productive and export capacity while foreign investments in association with local capital in large-scale iron, aluminum, and tourist industry projects increased.

In part as an ad hoc answer to the more severe consequences of the adjustment program itself and in part in response to its social concerns, the government initiated an ambitious social welfare program with the highly unusual approval of the IMF. The program included payments to needy families (a food grant), which was given to almost two million schoolchildren; a milk program for students; child-care assistance for mothers with breast-feeding infants; donations of clothing and school materials; a program for distributing rice and flour free of charge; day-care centers; credits for microbusinesses; half-fares on buses for students; obligatory insurance for those laid off from work; salary increases by presidential decree; meal and transportation vouchers for workers with low salaries; and an increase in both urban and rural minimum wages.

Despite the success of the Pérez government's macroeconomic programs and the ameliorative effects of these compensatory social welfare measures, opposition has been widespread. The government has not managed to form a coalition that can consolidate support for its ambitious reform program, not even among parts of the private sector that have been complaining for years about excessive state intervention.

The industrial sector fears a tariff reduction that will attract competition from abroad. The agricultural sector, facing elimination of subsidies on fertilizers, uncertainty produced by elimination of regulated and controlled prices, and the inevitability of import competition, complains about the lack of an agricultural policy. The financial sector resists a total opening of the economy that would permit the participation of foreign banks. This sector has benefited from the high annual interest rates on 90- and 180-day zero-coupon bonds provided by the Central Bank to absorb excess liquidity. However, it rejects an increase in legally required minimum bank reserves, accusing the government of stimulating inflation with excessive state expenditures while trying to brake inflation by draining funds from circulation with a restrictive monetary policy and high interest rates. The government is accused of both devaluing the bolivar to finance the fiscal deficit and simultaneously overvaluing it, thereby reducing the economy's capacity to export.

The unions complain that wage increases do not cover the rate of inflation, thus reducing the workers' real income, and that they have lost access to the government that they helped to elect. The government's

AD party complains about its diminished participation in the key ministerial jobs related to direction of the economy, insufficient ability to control social welfare programs that could generate political dividends, and the predominant role played by nonparty technocrats in the formulation and execution of an unpopular economic policy that weakens the electoral and patronage-distributing clout of the traditional system of pork-barrel politics.

Although the middle class received a subsidy through the housing law in order to compensate for the high rates of interest on mortgage loans, its level of consumption has slumped significantly. Access to automobiles, trips and shopping abroad, scholarships for students, and the rest of the privileges of the decade of the 1970s diminished and, for some, even disappeared.

All of this has been attributed to the corruption and inefficiency of the politicians and the parties that are now passing through a severe crisis of credibility and legitimacy. More optimistic observers regard this double economic and political crisis as an opportunity to reform the parties, the electoral system, and the state. It is seen as an opportunity for far-reaching reform that would increase the potential for participation and mobilization of the average citizen, putting an end to the almost monopolistic role of the parties in public life and giving the average citizen a greater voice in public affairs. Such popular participation could eliminate the paternalistic culture of patronage that has held the state, government, and party responsible for providing for everyone, and thus make the citizen assume direct personal responsibility for his or her own destiny and welfare.

Serious discussions about reducing the centralized power of party leaders to give a greater voice to the membership in guiding the party are being carried out within the parties themselves. The debate between orthodox sectors and those demanding renovation, between the older and younger generations, has permitted the establishment of an open forum regarding future leadership and new guidelines. This open confrontation of contrasting tendencies has challenged the old monolithic and highly disciplined system and, with it, the messianic and authoritarian leadership of the early years of democracy.

The direct election of governors and mayors on dates different from those for national elections has allowed the development of local leaders with their own power bases who are less indebted to the parties' national leaders. This development accompanies an increasing tendency to decentralize public administration through the transfer of power from the central government to the states and cities, a process constituting the beginning of a new federalism, though it is still in its infancy.

Outside party structure, citizens appear to be developing a new organizational spirit. Neighborhood associations, ecological groups, union elections with independent candidates, and frequent and occasionally spontaneous demonstrations and marches by groups demanding solutions to specific problems previously approached through party channels, are all poignant indications of this trend. Vociferous criticism of an electoral system in which national legislative candidates are voted for by party colors (or through a "uninominal" system) and not by the individual candidate's name (a "nominal" system) has provoked a growing demand for the establishment of nominal voting for the electoral college. The US model of districts for which a single representative is chosen has won many supporters, although this method eliminates proportional representation for minority parties, effectively disenfranchising the votes that do not go to the winner. This process would, as is well known, favor the two-party system and the largest parties. Nevertheless, the proposal for voting by the individual candidate's name is oriented toward diminishing the power of the parties and increasing the opportunities for nonprofessional politicians to access elected positions. Some noteworthy individuals might be favored by nominality. But the better-organized party machines and those with greater access to financing will probably benefit most, undoubtedly generating an enormous amount of disillusionment among those who envision the newly proposed electoral rules as a panacea in weakening the two-party oligopoly, and achieving a system in which elected leaders represent their constituencies better than their political parties.

Given that the two-party system has developed from the decisions of voters and not from a set of established rules, the emphasis placed on reform of the electoral rules to reduce the role of two-party politics may not produce the desired results. In creating new electoral districts it is easy to foresee the introduction of gerrymandering, a process made infamous by some states in the United States. Also, prevailing circumstances and attitudes favor the success of issue-oriented leadership—as opposed to legislative bodies that represent ideas, parties, ideologies, and programs—because voters are more concerned with specific improvements in the quality of life in areas such as the environment, food prices and supplies, public order, personal security, transportation, traffic control, garbage collection, an adequate water supply, and good telephone service. Local and municipal concerns have completely replaced any ideological concerns in much of the population's attitudes.

Both pragmatism and a reduction in dependence on ideologies are results of this distrust of politicians, combined with the fact that, although many of the initial political goals of the parties formulated more than thirty years ago were accomplished—they are no longer enough to satisfy contemporary popular demands. Today, there is no new program envisioned that is capable of mobilizing voters' loyalty and support. There is no dynamism to the system, even though it is based on free and direct

universal suffrage, on peaceful, alternating selection of leaders t(
clude the accumulation of power, and, despite the events of Feb
1992, on the rejection of military dictatorship. And the Cold war,
Castro's revolution, and conservative militarism are no longer menaces
that can serve as delegitimizing forces of democracy. In one sense, the
silent democratic revolution that since 1958 has transformed a poor,
rural Venezuela plagued by malaria and cronyism; produced a solid
urban, professional middle class; reduced illiteracy; filled the country
with schools, hospitals, and highways; built an important material infrastructure of paved roads, dams, and electric power lines; prepared a
framework for the development of small and medium industry and for
a relatively modern labor sector; and increased the number of universities tenfold—all under a system of reconciliation among society's elites,
paternalistic public expenditure, and patronage financed by oil money—
actually achieved the greater part of its economic and political goals. But
it neither succeeded in resolving problems of social inequalities nor in
broadening democratic representation. A healthy, constant rejuvenation
of the system has been missing.

The turmoil that followed the nearly successful military coup led by
Lt. Col. Hugo Chávez Frías on February 4, 1992, which would have erased
thirty-four years of democratically elected government, dramatically
highlights the serious deficiencies of the Venezuelan system and the
difficulties involved in attempting to change it for the better. One can
cite many factors that played a role in the coup attempt and the
overwhelming popular support shown for the plotters after their capture.
Two, however, appear to be central: frustration with the economic
situation and the failure of the political system to respond to the basic
demands of the population.

The program proposed by President Pérez's administration was
developed by his team of technocrats and was presented as the only
possible response to an economic crisis originating in the hypertrophy
of the state. But it has not succeeded in consolidating any fundamental
political support, either by making the immediate social costs of the
program more bearable or by legitimizing an economic program that
favors the free market system and the orientation of production toward
markets abroad. State reform is proceeding too slowly to produce public
support. Indeed, the lethargic pace of the reform has become another
cause of popular discontent.

The future pace, if not direction, of Venezuela's economic reform
program is in question today. The political crisis must be addressed in
tandem with economic questions. Among the obstacles to be overcome
is the continued resistance of business, politicians, labor leaders, scholars, and intellectuals, whose interests, ideology, and traditional, patron-
age-oriented political culture are all affected with each step forward. And

although the adjustment program's initial shock tactics produced rapid results in reestablishing equilibrium at the macroeconomic level, the continued application of policies of structural change that affect the privatization of state property, industrial reconversion, financial and fiscal reform, administrative, and electoral and political reforms are by their very nature slower in producing results.

The elections for municipal and gubernatorial posts in December 1992 will be an important test for Venezuela. The adjustment program's lack of popularity as a result of its social costs could produce a high rate of abstention and a significant defeat for the government. Even so, the leading opposition party, COPEI, potentially the principal beneficiary of the discontent, seems committed to supporting a continuation of the structural changes using the model that was so successful for the Christian Democrats in Germany. That model's goals were twofold: building a socially oriented market economy and realizing a state of law. Unlike the resistance of the labor unions and the traditional members of the government's own Social Democratic party, whose leadership accuses the government of having fallen victim to excessive neoliberal influence and the dictates of the International Monetary Fund, COPEI criticizes the government for its slow and inefficient application of this program. COPEI also criticizes the slow rate of the reconversion and privatization process, the inefficiency of the government's social welfare policies, corruption and the inability to control it, the contradictions between an expansive fiscal policy and a restrictive monetary policy, and the failure to control inflation sufficiently (although the rate has declined from 80 percent in 1989 to 35 percent in 1990 and about 30 percent in 1991). Significantly, however, COPEI does not object to the program itself.

As for the long-term, Carlos Andrés Pérez is as of this writing considered likely to remain in office until the presidential elections of 1993. If they produce a change in the governing party, there will likely be continuity in the essential policies for transforming the economy and the political system. The task of constructing an economy that is more open to foreign trade and investments, less protectionist, non-interventionist, increasingly diversified in its export trade, better equipped for international economic activity, more politically representative and participatory, less centralized, and, finally, more open to independent thinking, is an enormous one.

In the international arena, which will continue to have a strong domestic political and economic impact, Venezuela's policies have been extremely forward-looking, committed to defending the peace process in Central America, the strengthening of the United Nations, the defense of nuclear non-proliferation and human rights, and support of the United States by increasing oil production during the crisis in the Gulf. Venezuela also has been committed to the ratification of the international convention against drug trafficking, support for efforts to end the Cold War and deal effectively with its aftermath, the promotion of regional integration, the encouragement of free trade through participation in GATT, and support for President Bush's Enterprise for the Americas Initiative (EAI).

Nevertheless, Venezuela has found numerous obstacles on the road to gaining access to markets in the United States. The latent protectionist tendencies in various sectors of the US economy have produced strong threats of all kinds to erect barriers to trade with Venezuela. For example, the country has faced accusations of "dumping" Venezuelan cement at below-market prices, as well as restrictions on the purchase of tuna based on an accusation that Venezuelan fishermen kill too many dolphins. Trawlers have been fined for allegedly employing discriminatory practices against US vessels, and the United States has brought antidumping lawsuits against Venezuelan exports of aluminum and steel products. On the other hand, Venezuela has received very little help in the fight against drug trafficking relative to the aid that has been provided to Peru, Bolivia, and Colombia. The country has not received any recognition for having closed the gap in the international oil market produced by the loss of the four million barrels a day previously exported by Iraq and Kuwait. To do so, Venezuela had to increase its production drastically, almost to maximum capacity. Despite having resolved satisfactorily the foreign debt problem and having opened the economy to foreign investment, the US reaction has been minimal. Almost all financing for official programs has come from multinational organizations, not private investment bankers, except in the case of converting debt to capital.

In addition, the rejection of the Venezuelan initiative to forge an agreement between petroleum producers and consumers with the goal of preventing sudden variations in price and volume of oil deserves mention. Such a move would have restrained the harmful repercussions these variations cause in an increasingly interdependent international economy. Another unfortunate example is the slow rate of US free trade negotiations with Venezuela, despite President Pérez's support for the EAI, under the pretext that the United States, already too busy with Mexico, can only negotiate one agreement at a time. The increasing number of US non-tariff barriers to Venezuelan trade, justified on the grounds of health, ecology, and antidumping protection—after years of preaching that Venezuela should develop an open economy based on competitive advantages—appears to be a double standard. Venezuela's competitive advantages have been converted into unfair trading practices. The US is constantly pressuring Venezuela concerning matters that worry the Bush administration, such as the absence of laws that protect industrial patents and regulations that impede the exposure of the laundering of drug money. Yet there is a conspicuous absence of attention to the concerns of Venezuela, such as how to establish regulations that do not impede efforts to create an open financial system; to develop competitive, high-profit industries; and to secure licenses for such technology (even though it quickly becomes obsolete). How to build a competitive and open market economy that does not destroy the results of years of effort to create a local agricultural and industrial base, generate massive unemployment in the process, and debilitate democratic government is another major concern that the United States does not appear to appreciate.

Constructing a modern and competitive economy based on free market principles, open to international trade, capital, and investment, and capable of generating sustained growth with low rates of inflation is a slow and difficult process. It is even more trying to do this while developing a democratic, pluralistic, and increasingly representative and participatory political system that provides equal opportunity, greater equality in the distribution of incomes and wealth and allows greater individual initiative, self-esteem, and job training without such great dependence on government support. It is difficult to build democracy in conditions of crisis, inflation, unemployment, and poverty that are aggravated, even if temporarily, by the economic restructuring process itself—without eliminating civil liberties or succumbing to a repressive regime. Confusion, dissension, and turmoil are to be expected—and the events of February 4, 1992, have dramatically increased the pressure for results.

Thus, it is essential to forge a domestic political coalition committed to the transformation and to the assumption of the political and economic costs of the "Great Turnaround." It is necessary to obtain bilateral and multilateral cooperation from the international community. It is vital, moreover, that important official, business, and academic groups in countries such as the United States understand the magnitude of the challenge. It is also critical, finally, that these countries realize that Venezuelans share a deep faith in the ideals of democracy, economic development, and social justice—and deserve encouragement for their goals and aspirations—if they are to succeed.

In this spirit in June 1990 the Latin American Program of the Woodrow Wilson International Center for Scholars held a major conference, "Venezuelan Democracy and Political and Economic Change," which gave rise to this book. The conference brought together a diverse group of scholars and public officials from both Venezuela and the United States to discuss the process of political and economic reform in Latin America's second-oldest democracy. The participants included representatives of the Pérez government and the opposition, as well as US scholars who have closely studied the country for many years. Their examination of the first year of the new Venezuelan government, coupled with an epilogue detailing the circumstances surrounding the February 4, 1992, coup attempt, its implications, and the subsequent and ongoing crisis of governance, provides important insights for individuals who seek a better understanding of the reality of Venezuela today.

This book is composed of chapters based on papers or presentations by the Venezuelans at the conference, the edited transcripts of commentary on the conference panels and the discussion sessions that followed them, and material written specifically for the book.

Part 1 addresses the democratic development of Venezuela. In Chapter 1, Germán Carrera Damas, Venezuela's ambassador to Colombia and professor emeritus at the Central University of Venezuela, adopts a historical perspective. He views the development of Venezuelan democracy in three interrelated stages: the establishment of a sovereign liberal state, the shaping of the liberal democratic state, and the establishment of a democratic society. The first two stages were completed successfully, while the third is still in progress. After three decades of democratic government, according to Carrera Damas, Venezuelans fully understand that the broad democratization of society is indispensable to modernization.

In Chapters 2 and 3, David Myers, who has long studied and written extensively on Venezuela, and Larry Diamond, whose work has focused on politics and democracy in the developing world, comment on Carrera Damas's thesis. Myers argues that Venezuela, after some sluggishness, is now experiencing the revitalization of a system that functioned quite well for more than two decades. Venezuela's strength, he added, is its national parties, and when they undergo reform the reformers should be careful not to weaken them. But the country must also deal with the problems of institutional continuity, the younger generations' demands for access to leadership positions, and the need for judicial reform. Diamond argues that in order to implement the sweeping economic reform Venezuela needs, there must be a simultaneous process of democratization. The population must be educated to understand the reforms, and the government must receive popular input in the process. In this regard, Diamond believes that the rise of mass communication in politics could be an important tool for education, but it could also weaken political parties by allowing politicians direct access to the electorate.

Part 2 is devoted to an extensive discussion of Venezuela's economic evolution, focusing on the traumatic period from 1989 to 1991. In Chapter 4, Moisés Naím, minister of development during the first year of the Pérez administration and former executive director of the World Bank, provides an in-depth analysis of the government's radical economic program. He addresses the justification for the "Great Turnaround," its implementation, its consequences, and the lessons to be learned from the experience.

Venezuela, Naím argues, requires a deeper ideological foundation for the economic reforms being implemented, but policy stability will not come without "a stronger, more efficient state." Naím concludes that three deeply rooted characteristics of the Venezuelan state must be addressed before the state's developmental possibilities can improve: (1) use of the public bureaucracy as a functional substitute for the absence of a safety net for the unemployed; (2) the political role assigned to public employment, the lack of trained personnel, and poor working conditions in the public sector; and (3) the lack of sufficient capacity for autonomous action by the state. The ultimate challenge, Naím writes, is to build a state "capable of defending the interest of the unorganized majority against the voraciousness of highly organized and influential minorities."

Part 3 considers the Venezuelan experience in both regional and international perspectives. In Chapter 5, Carlos Blanco, who guided the reforms as minister of State and president of the Presidential Commission for State Reform (COPRE), places Venezuela within the context of the reform movement across Latin America. He stresses that regional economic problems cannot be separated from political and social crises, and that they cannot be resolved without an integral transformation of the society and state. Blanco discusses six areas that must be addressed: political reforms, decentralization, administrative modernization, modernization of the state of law, modernization of public policies, and the development of civil society.

In Chapter 6, Beatrice Rangel, former foreign policy advisor to President Pérez and his representative on several key diplomatic missions, focuses on Venezuela's role in the world. Shortcomings in the political system, she writes, led Venezuela's foreign policy makers to look abroad to relieve some the country's problems. This new approach was intially aimed at curbing drug trafficking, resolving Central American conflicts, and strengthening Latin American policy coordination in international economic relations. Most important, according to Rangel, is that today the new foreign policy design takes the interests of foreign investors and, for the first time, the private sector into account.

The commentary of Sally Shelton-Colby, who has focused on the Caribbean region over a long period of time, first as deputy assistant secretary of state and ambassador, then as a professor and consultant, is provided in Chapter 7. She emphasizes the importance of strong democratic institutions and processes. Moreover, she argues, economic democracy—the promotion of development as well as growth—is critical to the reform process and something on which US policy must place greater emphasis. Venezuela, she adds, does not receive the credit it deserves for the substantial reforms it has adopted.

Venezuelan politics and policymaking are the topics of Part 4. Andrés Stambouli, a veteran student of the political process as a member of faculty at the Central University of Venezuela (UCV), and also a former advisor to COPRE, evaluates the first year of the Pérez government in Chapter 9. If there is anything to be learned from the first year, according to Stambouli, "it is that communications between the government and society have changed significantly as far as the government decisionmaking process is concerned, both in form and content." Venezuelan democracy is adapting to the changing times, he argues; the protective democracy of the early 1970s has become a mature democracy. Changes in the form of governing, the manner in which the opposition is manifested, and the way the public expresses itself augurs well for "positive and even more profound" changes in the quality of that democracy over the medium term.

In Chapter 10, Gustavo Tarre Briceño discusses the role of the opposition party COPEI during this period of reform. A COPEI deputy and congressional leader dedicated to reform and modernization, Tarre describes how Venezuelans grew tired of the statist, two-party system established in 1958 to the point where it became a crisis. The popular consensus disappeared. Tarre emphasizes, however, that the elected opposition at the state and national level must not be extremist; it must not be a confrontational impediment to government action. Rather it should be open to mutual understandings, which suggests government-requested assistance from the opposition, aimed at promoting the public good through a long-term policy approach. Tarre supports some of the steps taken by Pérez, but notes flaws in his program.

In Chapter 11, the commentary of John Martz, a US scholar of Venezuela who has written extensively about the country, addresses the role of the party system since 1958 and notes that despite its weaknesses it has functioned remarkably well. With regard to parties, a new era is beginning in Venezuela. According to Martz, notwithstanding the current problems—the need for reform and the need for changes in operation—"there is a demonstrated capacity on the part of the political parties and of the party elites in Venezuela to respond." Ultimately, there will be a somewhat different political system, but the parties will maintain their central role.

In Chapter 12, Diego Abente, also a US scholar of Venezuela, adds that the profound changes under way need to be accomplished without sacrificing the democratic and participatory decisionmaking style of the first Pérez administration The process of change reflects the modernization of a more complex Venezuelan society. Abente is reluctant to differentiate between the political and the programmatic styles of Venezuelan politics, because ultimately, though there will be changes in the mode of operation, the basic function of politics—the distribution of rewards—will remain constant.

Part 5 is an epilogue, included with the aim of updating Venezuela's political and economic situation. In Chapter 14, Moisés Naím provides

17

a detailed chronological analysis of events surrounding the attempted coup of February 4, 1992. He addresses its causes and analyzes the lessons to be drawn from the experience of the past three years. According to Naím, a few critical lessons stand out for future policymakers: the need to strengthen public institutions, link macroeconomic stabilization with basic public services, and communicate with individuals, groups, and organizations about economic policy reforms. "It would be a grievous mistake," he also writes, "to conclude that the state of the economy was the fundamental force underlying the Venezuelan political and institutional crisis."

At the conclusion of each panel of the Venezuela conference there was a period of discussion. The edited transcripts of these sessions are provided after the commentary chapters in an effort to record the particular issues raised. They may prove to be of special interest to the reader.

Note

Gary Bland, program associate of the Latin American Program of the Woodrow Wilson International Center for Scholars, edited the translated text and wrote the chapter summaries.

PART 1

VENEZUELA'S DEMOCRATIC DEVELOPMENT

1

Venezuelan Democracy in Historical Perspective

Germán Carrera Damas

The history of Venezuela, as seen from today's vantage point, reveals a sense of the formation of a democratic society as an objective, a historical task, and an end. It is most important to stress these *three circumstances*, because the first reveals the perspicacity in choosing the road to be followed toward its social goals; the second shows the tenacity and perseverance demonstrated in following that road; and the third tells us not only the results, but above all indicates a consciousness of the reality of the achievements attained after almost two centuries of toil. The formation of a democratic society in Venezuela does not differ greatly from that of the United States after two hundred years, slowed to a considerable extent by the weight of racism; or from that of France following two centuries dotted with authoritarian eruptions.

It is possible to identify three major stages in the life of the Venezuelan people, who determined their own destiny after severing colonial ties with the Spanish metropolis, following a long and bloody war that decimated more than a third of its population, considerably damaged the economic base of the country, and eroded the civilization and culture that had evolved over the three preceding centuries.

The first stage was organically linked to the war of independence. The declaration of independence itself and the promulgation of the Federal Constitution of 1811 had already given form to the objective of installing a sovereign state structured along the constitutional norms of liberalism. The dispute over federalism or centralism, as seen from today's perspective, appears to have been between conservative liberals and reformist liberals, but the differences actually lay in the social agendas of the disputants. The sole purpose of the ruling class was to reestablish the internal structure of power that had been damaged by the war. What actually established the difference between the two factions was the debate over whether to continue the efforts of preserving and consolidating the arduously reestablished internal power structure, or to use adjustments and changes that would allow the state to channel, and

Germán Carrera Damas is ambassador to Colombia for the Republic of Venezuela.

21

thus regulate, the social conflicts that had led to the struggle for liberty and equality of the various social sectors or classes. I refer to the struggle of the criollos for equality with respect to the peninsular Spaniards, to the struggle of the mulattos for equality with respect to the criollos, and to the struggle of the slaves for liberty with respect to the defenders of slavery. Waged in a variety of theaters, these struggles were fought throughout colonial Venezuelan society and persisted in the independent republic, the latter two struggles in a quite obvious fashion, with the criollos constituting one of the poles in both of those struggles.

The confrontation between these political conceptions, following a bloody five-year war known as the Federal War, led to the second stage: the shaping of the democratic liberal state. Indeed, the emphasis was no longer on the constitutional form but rather on the purpose of, and mechanisms for, shaping political power. Suffrage was invalidated in practice by the establishment of a sort of single-party regime. The Liberal party had proved victorious in the war due to the virtual dissolution of the defeated Conservative party and the absorption by the former of many of the followers of the latter. Events served to firmly establish the democratic enlargement of the liberal state, from which it was no longer possible to retreat except on the basis of the de facto situations that discouraged the formation of modern political parties. In the social order of things, two very important long-term results were achieved: (1) the road was closed to the return of privileges, and (2) bases were established for a lay state as a consequence of the rupture of the economic, social, and political power of the Catholic church, the formation of the Organization for Public Administration, and the decree of free, public, and mandatory primary education. Though it restrained political development, the prolonged autocracy of Antonio Guzmán Blanco from 1870 to 1886 deliberately and effectively promoted the liberalization of society, thus opening the way for its subsequent democratization.

It had been only a little less than one hundred years since the constitutional formulation of the democratic liberal state in 1864, but its postulates awaited a social development that only began to appear in 1930. With the thrust of the oil industry, the middle class developed, the working class was formed, and the state was provided with the resources and power necessary to advance the foundation of democratic social development and education, improvement of sanitary conditions, interregional linkages, and so on. Shaping a democratic society required the institutionalization of the democratic liberal state, only possible by means of the combative democratization of society: the organization of politics and labor into parties and labor unions, the unionization of the education sector, and the struggle for freedom of information. Thus were drawn the two correlative aspects of the third stage: the institutionalization of the democratic liberal state. This stage entered its implementation phase in 1945–1948 in a provisional fashion, and then again beginning in 1958. The constitutions of 1947 and 1961 in turn formulated and gave shape to the program for the democratization of society.

The stages that make up the Venezuelan national project, which could be expressed as the search for a democratic liberal sovereign state, pertain to the social whole, inasmuch as they are not the work of a party or governing group, but rather of a society moving toward specific purposes. The formulation of that project falls to a socially dominant class or sector, but although it meshes perfectly with the very interests of the sector or class that formulates it, it cannot help but correspond to some very basic degree to the interests of those sectors or classes that occupy a subordinate position, albeit interdependent, in the internal power structure. If this were not the case, the project could not be self-sustaining. The articulation of various social sectors or classes in the internal power structure is the end result of the critical confrontation of individuals, groups, and classes over time. The resistance to change and social transformation displayed by the actors is expressed not only as opposition to, but also as the active defense of, interests. Thus the historian cannot assign clear values to the effects of participation by conservative or reformist liberals in the formulation and promotion of the national project. This approach allows us to capture and appreciate the role played by each force or sector in these confrontations and even in armed conflicts.

The first stage of the Venezuelan national project was the establishment of a sovereign liberal state. In order to carry it out, it was necessary for Venezuelan society to take three giant and organically interrelated steps. The first was severing colonial ties with Spain, which was carried out during the 1821–1824 period. However, the resolve to carry out that severance, in terms of the desire to take action, was already in place at the time of the signing of the declaration of independence on July 5, 1811. It does not matter that some signed grudgingly; that others, upon signing, denied it later out of fear for the future; or that others subsequently conspired actively against what they had signed. Historians can always argue—to the health of our profession—about the deepest roots of the initial and primary act of sovereignty, about whether it expressed the will of an entire people or whether it was imposed by a small group of hotheads. But the social confrontation and bellicose clash unleashed during this first step ended up fulfilling perfectly the aspirations of the Venezuelan social whole.

The second step—abolition of the monarchy—was not necessarily implicit in the first, nor was it an indispensable or unavoidable precondition for severing colonial ties. Although it was politically necessary to do so at the critical juncture of the actual severance, it did not signify the need to completely abandon the monarchy as a form of social and

23

political organization. The Venezuelan people had proved themselves a genuinely monarchical people, both in their opposition to the intentions of other monarchs as well as in their repudiation of those who, like Francisco Miranda, would have induced them to sever their colonial ties. The obstinacy of Fernando VII in 1814, and the invasion of Spain by the sons of San Luis in 1823, closed the door on the constitutional monarchy—the original legacy of the French Revolution. Overcoming the mandates of the monarchical conscience, intimately linked as they were to the commandments of Catholic conscience, was a difficult task for all Venezuelans, not only for those like Juan Germán Roscio, who poured out his feelings in a book that today seems to us as confused and filled with tortuous theological-philosophical pathways as it was with its authentic and profound crisis of conscience. It was equally difficult for the thousands of illiterate citizens who saw in the rupture of the colonial ties and in the abandonment of the monarchy not only an act of disobedience to the will of the king but also, and above all, a disobedience to the will of God.

This firm resolve of a society in its goal to determine its own destiny has been minimized by the need of the historiography of independence, as well as that of the republic, to underestimate our monarchical past in order to legitimize our independence, but also, and especially, to exonerate us from the accusation of felony brought against us by the defenders of the king, whether peninsular Spaniards or Venezuelan criollos. The fact is that on July 19, 1810, we swore before God to defend the rights of Fernando VII and on July 5, 1811, we abolished the monarchy when, also before God, we declared our independence and established the republic. This historiographical modesty has led us to see ourselves as "never truly monarchical," if not as republicans *avant la lettre*.

The third step was building the republic, identified for this purpose with the establishment of the liberal state. If the preceding steps were difficult, this one was even more so: It was no longer a matter of demolishing something that existed but rather of replacing it with the realization of a concept. Colonial ties and the monarchy belonged to the realm of the deprivation of liberty. History shows that the paths leading to freedom are not always laid out by freedom itself. The construction of the republic clashed with the adverse republican experience both in France and the United States. Thus, Venezuelans threw themselves into the task of constructing the liberal republic, a task in which the Europeans had already failed and for which the North Americans had carved out an imperfect solution. Here it should be noted that indigenous societies have never been republican societies, nor are they so today. US historians have often perceived faults in the liberal republican foundation of the United States, faults similar to those that plagued Latin America during the nineteenth century. Both in the United States and in Latin America it took a long time to comprehend that it was not enough to sever colonial ties and abolish the monarchy to be able to have republics filled with free and equal citizens. Simón Rodríguez warned of this in 1828, and it garnered for him an intellectual exile that has lasted almost two centuries.

With the resolution of the fundamental problem produced by the war of independence—that of reestablishing the internal power structure, and removing the popular masses from the history of Venezuela in virtue of the political, not military, triumph of reformist liberalism in the Federal War (1859–1863)—there arose the needs to (1) consolidate the internal power structure by channeling the basic social conflict; and (2) propitiate the modernizing development of the internal power structure by opening the way to the transformation of the dominant class into a "European-style" middle class. Such was the goal of the liberalizing directed by the "civilizing autocrat" Antonio Guzmán Blanco and several of his illustrious collaborators.

In order to attain that objective, it was necessary to put together what I classify as the first systematic attempt to establish a democratic liberal state in Venezuelan society. The most novel aspect of this attempt was that it did not stop with the design of the necessary legal framework, but was actually put into practice. By providing Venezuelan society with a legal-doctrinal point of reference, the establishment and scope of which stood firm, two important results were achieved: (1) It was proved that it was indeed possible to escape from the stagnation in which Venezuelan society found itself beginning in the latter part of the eighteenth century; and (2) That society was given a modernizing model that had been lacking up until that point and which, though largely imitative in nature, did not entirely divest it of its potential. The demolition of the relics of the colonial regime, which had not only survived the severance of colonial ties but had even gained strength to the point of discrediting the subsequent republic, led to fierce resistance from powerful social sectors. The confrontation with the church, the exaltation—albeit more rhetorical than real—of things popular; and the preaching of liberalism in all of the various manifestations of society, were concepts that nurtured attitudes and intentions even among the closest collaborators of the "civilizing autocrat" who, in reacting against the despotic excesses of the autocrat, reduced the scope of the reforms undertaken without eliminating them altogether, with the result that they were left to form the basis for new developments.

The stage that I have characterized as a confrontation of the democratic liberal state consisted of the search for an equilibrium—certainly no simple task—between the modernizing, democratic, liberal proposal and the autocratic modernizing reformism. The difficulty lay in the fact that the reestablishment of the internal power structure, disjointed as a consequence of the war of independence, was not enough in itself to enable society to chart a new course. The absence of social, political, and economic structures was an expression of the marked weakness of a small ruling class lacking the power and the means to exercise its recently regained control over society and convert it into the power to orient that society. Concomitantly, a new European imperialist expansion, driven by the so-called second industrial revolution, gave birth to a modernizing wave that very soon created repercussions in Venezuela and provided liberal reformists with a point of reference that was as attractive as it was prestigious. Thus were created the conditions necessary for a sort of enlightened bossism, or caudillismo, excellently represented by Antonio Guzmán Blanco. The result was a startling dissociation between political life, in which the modernized liberal appearance scarcely covered up a bossist, autocratic exercise of power, and a modernizing liberal administration, no longer inducing but rather imposing social change. This "traditional" characteristic of reformism sparked annoyance and opposition even among those essentially identified with modernizing liberalism, but who in fact contributed significantly to the weight of the historical invariants, although in this case they manifested more as a reluctance toward change than as a doctrinal defense of the past, an attitude that brought the definitive abandonment of conservatism as a political doctrine.

The urgency to generate social and economic forces capable of sustaining and driving the democratic liberal project still prevails in Venezuelan society, fed by disoriented Marxist historiography, a feeling of resentment with respect to the "civilizing autocrat" who made us aware of the backwardness and primitivism prevailing in our society. The democratizing liberal project constituted the beginning of an important Venezuelan tradition: the pedagogical exercise of power along the lines of, or perhaps as an imitation of, the enlightened despotism of which Europe has given us so many examples. Antonio Guzmán Blanco knew quite well that this project could not be fully realized in the Venezuelan society of his time unless it became possible to launch that society on a course of economic and cultural strengthening. Therefore, in his opinion, the decision to open the doors to European capital was as necessary for the progress of the country as it was lucrative for his own personal interests.

During the first part of the nineteenth century, progress was a notion linking all things material, political, social, and moral. The autocratic exercise of public power led to a crude differentiation between material progress and everything else, with the former claiming priority for itself and justifying the abandonment of all other dimensions of progress. The latter part of the nineteenth century, as well as almost the first four decades of the twentieth, were spent on that debate, represented most ably by Juan Vicente Gómez. But who could suspect that material progress, brought about in this case by the advent of the petroleum civilization, would necessarily lead to the proposal for the need to return to the social, political, and moral arenas the areas of purview that rightfully belonged to them? Hence, beginning in 1936, the struggle for democratization was introduced with the sense of promoting the establishment of a democratic society wherein those dimensions abandoned by progress would recover their validity.

Not surprisingly, the trend initiated by Antonio Guzmán Blanco was resumed. I say this with the knowledge that it would not have occurred to those who provided a new driving force to that trend to proclaim themselves as perpetuators of the "civilizing autocrat," for they expressly considered themselves the antithesis of all he had so negatively represented. But beginning in 1945, power was consecrated to defining, deciding, and promoting the democratization of Venezuelan society, an objective considered prerequisite for preventing new autocracies and promoting modernization. With lacunae, periods of stagnation on some occasions, and attempts to back down on others, this concept of the exercise of public power has prevailed up to the present time. The state has assumed the role of an agent promoting democratization and modernization, with its political will making up for the still notorious insufficiency of its social, economic, and cultural structures and substituting for them in the establishment of goals. But we must make no mistake when evaluating this function of the state: It has found an echo and enjoyed the support of a society whose participation through the exercise of suffrage has left no room for doubt. In this sense, Venezuelan society has proved more lucid than many sectors of political, economic, and even cultural life for which the exercise of democracy remains problematic.

How is it possible to reconcile the goal of establishing a democratic society in the absence of social structures intrinsically predisposed to such an occurrence, and in a situation in which the state assumes a guiding, substitutive function? One possible explanation lies in the fact that beginning in 1936 the Venezuelan state entered into a period of growth in its economic power as a result of the legally constituted regime of oil exploration, the end result being that whoever controls the state controls society. This seeming platitude begins to make sense when "control" is not only interpreted as "rule" but particularly as the power to shape society, because the latter still lacks the ability to manage its own affairs.

After more than three decades of the institutionalized exercise of democracy in the political system, it is now finally understood that the profound and broad democratization of society is an indispensable prerequisite for pursuing the modernization effort. And it has also finally been understood that modernization is a precondition for increasing the breadth and depth of democratization. This is not a mere play on words—it is an indication of the conceptual knot faced today by Venezuelan society after comprehending that one can modernize and even democratize the political system from a position of power, but one cannot do the same to society. We can open the way for society, but movement has to come from within society itself if we are to achieve a genuine and self-sustaining result, one capable of looking out for its own preservation.

Perhaps an example will aid in better understanding this point. The shaping of democratic society in the United States remained incomplete until the 1960s, when that country began to implement significant consecutive measures aimed at attenuating and eventually eliminating the weight of racism that so characterized its society. The traditional approach has been to omit this fact by classifying US society as democratic, or to lessen its importance by stressing the nondemocratic aspects of our society. In Venezuela the process of overcoming racial discrimination as a manifest and recognized basis of society has been more the work of society itself than of the state, and this is one of the few areas in which the constitutional norm has simply served to legitimize social practice. This odious obstacle, which undergirded our social structure up to the time of the congresses of Colombia and the Federal War, was overcome by the process of social dynamics. Today we can say that ours is a democratic society that is not defined by racism, even on a sectoral basis—even though the practice of racism lingers to a certain degree as it does in every known democratic society.

One of the characteristics of contemporary Venezuelan society has been the lag between historical conscience and social conscience. We continue to live the fundamental portion of our history on the basis of nineteenth-century criteria. But it would appear that as regards the relationship between modernization and democratization, we have produced, purely by virtue of political conscience, the elimination of that lag, and the current proposal with regard to the reform of the Venezuelan state is totally congruent with the current historical moment of society. By this I mean that current endeavors to reform the state are not inspired by goals of a single individual, group, or class—rather, they express a powerful historical determinant. Venezuelan society, having successfully completed the first two stages of its national project, shall be equally successful with regard to the third; and not too far into the coming century, it will be truly democratic.

2

Commentary

David Myers

What has been expressed with regard to political and economic reform is that dramatic changes are being made in a system that had functioned very well in many respects for more than two decades. For example, the issue of decentralization raises the question of why there had been so much centralization in Venezuela. The nineteenth century was a nightmare of regional revolts and the political system at the center was designed to hold it together. The twentieth century began in Venezuela with concern as to whether the system would hold together or not. Also, the discovery of oil tended to reinforce centralization and control by the Caracas government.

Although much has been done to reduce dependence on oil, one of the outstanding characteristics of the last fifteen years is that oil has become so important that it has brought about even greater centralization. Thus one has to realize that the attempt to decentralize runs against the trend of almost 150 years of Venezuelan politics and political development. It is difficult to make such an abrupt shift in a short period of time. People have to change the way they think. Therefore, it is not surprising that the first elections under the new system saw over 50 percent abstention, in a situation designed to link voters to political choices in a new way. This seems an important challenge for the Venezuelan political elite, for the strengthening of democracy, and perhaps for the very survival of the Venezuelan democratic regime.

One can see in Venezuela that when the distribution system worked well, the centralized democratic system got a great deal of credit for it. Indeed, it was one of the things that allowed consolidation of the democratic system. On the other hand, when those resources were no longer there to work with and things did not go well, central government also had to take the blame for that; one result was the rioting in late February 1989, less than a month after Carlos Andrés Pérez had taken over the presidency. So one of the challenges or benefits of centralization is that the people have more pressure points by which they gain influence

David Myers is professor of political science at Pennsylvania State University.

29

over the government.

Venezuela has had the good fortune to have political parties that are truly national. Were it not for Acción Democrática, and were it not for the expansion of the party system under the leadership of Rómulo Betancourt, there would be no democracy in Venezuela, which reversed more than a century of dictatorial tradition. One can see that the Venezuelan party confiscated the state apparatus. But in another sense, that confiscation may have been absolutely critical in terms of the establishment of democracy.

No modern democracy functions well without strong political parties. When attempts are made to reform parties, it is important that there not be an overall weakening of them. It could be argued that if political parties are indiscriminately weakened, the way is open for reassertion of a militaristic tradition. However, the fact of our not wanting to weaken parties indiscriminately should not be taken to mean that Venezuela's political parties are not in need of a certain amount of reform.

There is the problem of lifelong positions in Venezuela's political leadership. There are clearly new generations waiting to move up; the question is, Can channels be provided for these young people? If one generation controls the political process for too long, it loses its vitality and may eventually lose its ability to control the government. One can see in both of the major political parties in Venezuela that some of the people who played heroic roles in the establishment of democracy are still in leadership positions. In certain instances this has led to splits that clearly require some adjustment. is it the role of the state to force that adjustment? To what degree can that adjustment be legislated by Congress and to what degree must it come out of the political party system itself? Perhaps the state ought to keep a hands-off policy and allow for a Darwinian approach in which those political parties most successful in bringing vigorous new leadership are indeed the ones that triumph.

Another question is the modernization of public administration—the idea that bureaucracies often lose their institutional continuity, particularly between changes of government. While this happens to a certain extent in all countries, in Venezuela and in many Latin American countries it happens even more—a new minister and a new team comes in and they totally undo everything that the previous government did, whether good or bad. The result is that policies are not put into operation until the second or third year of the new administration. Then there is only a year and a half for those policies to take effect before the start of the new election campaign, to which all energy is then directed. Clearly this is a major problem in Venezuelan public administration, a problem that, looking back at the petro-bonanza years, tended to impede the most effective use of the great resources that came in during that period.

During the guerrilla warfare period of democratic consolidation in

Venezuela, the judiciary was extremely politicized as a means of stopping the guerrillas from using it to escape or to protect their movement. However, the politicization of the judicial system gave rise to the idea that there was no impartial enforcement of regulations and laws. To undertake certain structured reforms, such as campaign disclosure laws, there must be an independent judiciary to actually enforce laws and punish those who have broken them.

We can have hope for the revitalization of a system that performed heroically, making an almost 90-degree turn in the political evolution of Venezuela between 1958 and 1980. Since 1980, it has been rather sluggish in adjusting to a new range of realities. How the people, the politicians, and the decisionmakers adjust to these new realities will determine not only the viability of the democratic system for whose creation so many suffered, but also the quality of that democratic system and the quality of life of the average Venezuelan.

3

Commentary

Larry Diamond

First, a cautionary note about the applicability of the Venezuelan experience. As David Myers suggests, Venezuela not only has a certain disequilibrium that necessitated reform, but also has certain advantages that facilitated it. The most obvious advantage is thirty years of a relatively well-functioning and institutionalized democracy, despite all the problems of inefficiency and favoritism that required reform. There was a reserve of legitimacy that could be drawn upon. Rather daring and painful steps could be taken with relative assurance that democracy would not collapse the next day, that the whole infrastructure of freedom would not cave in due to massive popular rejection. It should be noted that this same reservoir of institutional continuity, strength, and legitimacy does not exist in Eastern Europe, nor does it exist in some of the new troubled or renewed democracies, such as Argentina and Peru.

It should also be observed that democracies can implement sweeping structural adjustments. There are two ways to tear apart and reconstruct an economy as burdened with structural inefficiencies and contradictions as is that of Venezuela. One is a democratic way, and the other the authoritarian method General Pinochet used in Chile—absolutely repressing any popular protest and completely unconcerned with popular resistance and pain, with the conviction that the eventual reconstruction will be so successful that people will be grateful that it was done, even if they still resent that it was done so repressively and unjustly.

Therefore, if a true democracy is to pursue this type of sweeping structural adjustment, it has to do it democratically. This then raises the issue of the relationship between economic and political reforms. It is not just these two processes that we need to be concerned with, but also the way they interact with each other. We need to question whether economic reform could be so successful and so tolerated in Venezuela if there was not a simultaneous process of democratization. There must be popular input and popular education to get people to accept within a

Larry Diamond is senior research fellow at The Hoover Institution on War, Revolution and Peace at Stanford University.

democratic framework the level of short-term pain, sacrifice, and dislocation that accompanies this level of restructuring. To what extent have attempts been made to educate the Venezuelan people about economic realities and to tear down thirty years of myth about state populism, which led people to expect state favors as their democratic right? Interestingly, in the past year or two and well before the recent presidential election in Argentina, the women's democratic education group, Conciencia, an idea that began in Argentina and has now spread throughout most of South America, adopted as a major priority the task of educating ordinary citizens about economics. They recognized that reform would be impossible unless people could be reeducated to understand the elementary economic principles of a competitive economy and the ultimate destructiveness of favoritism and protection.

The economic restructuring of an economy as badly wounded as Venezuela's cannot be pursued piecemeal and incrementally. There needs to be a relatively sweeping and simultaneous attack on all fronts. We have seen why price structure, foreign exchange, interest rates, and the structure of ownership and employment are so intrinsically related that a change in one, particularly beginning with prices, has profound implications for everything else.

We can think of democracy as involving three dimensions: (1) extensive popular participation; (2) meaningful competition for power positions that really matter in society; and (3) liberty, a set of freedoms of expression, organization, assembly, and beliefs meaningful enough to actualize democracy. It is interesting that COPRE is attacking every dimension of this conception of democracy. We must realize that democracy is not something that a country either has or does not have, although that is the way we tend to think of it. Rather, democracy is a continuum, and we can think of each of these three dimensions of democracy—competition, participation, and liberty—as reaching varying levels of inclusiveness, authenticity, and meaning.

When parties are encouraged to open up and to use democratic nominating processes, competition deepens. The popular election of governors and mayors is itself one of the most important and necessary developments for the improvement of democratic competition. One of the most profound lessons I have learned through a comparative study of more than two dozen developing countries is that decentralization of power is not only an intrinsic element of democracy, but also one of the most impressive correlates of a legitimate and well-functioning democracy. The steps that have been taken to decentralize power are going to pay very rich dividends in Venezuela.

On the Freedom House scale that rates countries from 1 for the most democratic to 7 for the most authoritarian, Venezuela is one of only two countries in the world—the other is the Dominican Republic—that rates a 1 with regard to political competition, but it receives a 3 with regard to civil liberties, which is surprising for a "full" democracy. This implies that there are problems with the rule of law, the judiciary, and freedom of expression that need institutional attention.

There is a sad tendency among people and scholars to assume that we are a "developed" democracy and therefore have lessons to teach other countries. This is a particular problem with some of the efforts that emerge with missionary zeal from our official and semiofficial structures to promote and finance the development of democracy around the world. It is important to appreciate that democracy is a developing phenomenon. Every generation confronts new obstacles to liberty and the freedom and fullness of competition, new disincentives and obstructions to participation, and every democracy has to continue to adapt to changing circumstances.

"Established" democracies, such as those in the United States and Europe, may have something to learn from the far-reaching, daring, and impressive effort at political reform and reevaluation that is going on now in Venezuela. For example, we have not solved the problem of party financing, which remains a grotesque handicap in achieving the democratic goals of our political system. Something on the order of 97 percent of all incumbents in the House of Representatives who run for reelection are reelected. How competitive is that?

One of the conditions that democracies need to adapt to is the changing level of communications. We are now in an age of stunning transformation of our whole system of communication—its decentralization, increasing speed, internationalization, and so on—with major implications for the way politics is conducted. I am afraid the new technologies will weaken political parties as traditional grassroots organizing institutions. On the other hand, they will also facilitate the capacity of party leaders and government officials to communicate with and educate the public in responsible ways. We need to think about how television and other modern communication systems can be used not to obfuscate public understanding, but to facilitate democratization and draw people into the process.

An absolute prerequisite for true democratic competition in a modern television age is that competing parties receive free public access to television air time during a campaign. That this is not the case, in my judgment, is a disgraceful impediment to political competition in the United States. This is the primary reason why political campaigns have become so expensive and political parties so dependent on special-interest financing. It would be interesting to know what COPRE has done or is considering doing with regard to free access, both for established parties and for new ones that might receive a percentage of the vote by receiving television and radio air time. This may reduce the cost and time

35

necessary for campaigns, and may also produce more responsible campaigns.

PART 2

THE ECONOMIC TRANSFORMATION

4

The Launching of Radical Policy Changes, 1989–1991

Moisés Naím

What makes a country adopt a radically different economic policy? What factors intervene in the execution of reforms and what are the obstacles to their effective implementation? Which factors impel adoption of a shock treatment method of policy reform and which make reforms more gradualistic? Are we witnessing one more wave of the periodic adjustments imposed on these countries by international economic circumstances, or are these reforms permanent? What is the political economy of policy reversals?

Although the experience of the many countries that in the 1980s and early 1990s have adopted new and essentially similar, market-centered policy orientations is still too recent and has been too varied to provide unequivocal and universal answers to the above questions, preliminary evidence seems to point to significant parallels and shared experiences. The following pages will attempt to shed some light on these questions by analyzing the recent experience of Venezuela in shaping and launching the most radical economic policy change ever attempted in its history. Thus, this chapter has two main purposes: (1) to document the antecedents, the launching process, and the preliminary results of the adoption by Venezuela of a market-oriented policy package of macroeconomic stabilization and structural change; and (2) to distill from that experience some more general implications.

We start by summarizing Venezuela's recent economic evolution, emphasizing the conditions that eventually made the adoption of such radical changes possible. After discussing the specific problems that the country was facing on the eve of the radical policy changes, we present the basic traits of the reform program and then describe its launching process. We then review the initial effects of the reforms and conclude by turning to some of the main lessons and more general implications that can be derived from this experience.

Moisés Naím is senior associate of the Carnegie Endowment for International Peace.

The Inverted Midas Touch: A Glimpse into
Venezuela's Recent Economic Evolution

For decades, virtually all one needed to know about the Venezuelan economy could be summed up in one word: oil. Oil became the dominant feature of Venezuela's economic profile in the 1920s. And despite the dramatic policy shift in 1989, a primary goal of which was to promote economic diversification, Venezuela in the midnineties and for the foreseeable future will, in all likelihood, remain dependent on the oil industry. Oil, for example, is responsible for more than 70 percent of all government revenue and more than 80 percent of all the foreign exchange earnings of the country.

Oil brought Venezuela to the pinnacle of economic success, but it did not spare the country the depths of economic crisis. During the 1950s and 1960s, oil exports provided the country with the possibility of having one of the most successful economies in the world. Compounded annual growth averaged a remarkable 6 percent during this twenty-year period.[1]

As the oil industry matured, Venezuela, a country that once based its living on a small pastoral-agriculture sector, developed an extractive mining economy with a substantial capacity to generate foreign exchange earnings. Most of these earnings were accrued by the government, which in turn reinvested and spent them, attempting to both alleviate poverty and diversify the economy.

The boom, however, eventually turned to bust. Heavy reliance on a single highly profitable export product inhibited adoption of a policy orientation that could have avoided the long-term decline in productivity and economic health that began just as the boom reached its height. Ultimately, the vagaries of the world oil market and the weak foundation underlying the economy forced a change in course. In 1989 the newly elected government of Carlos Andrés Pérez launched a structural economic overhaul—starting what probably will be a very different era for Latin America's fourth-largest economy.

The exploitation of the country's oil began in the 1920s. Some of the major consequences of the rapid development of the oil industry were the displacement of agriculture as the core sector of the economy, which in turn sparked the fastest urbanization process on the continent, a heavy reliance of the public sector on oil to finance its activities, and, as a consequence, a very low incentive to search for other sources of revenue. This last trend continued until the late 1950s, when the new democratic regime adopted the classic import-substitution industrialization scheme with the purpose of creating an industrial base that could eventually provide some degree of diversification to the economy.

Venezuela was the latest of the large countries in the region to initiate

Table 4.1   The Period of Oil Price Stability, 1952–1973

Average Yearly Inflation	1.7%
Average Yearly Rate of Growth	6.0%

Source: CORDIPLAN

a systematic industrialization effort. Nonetheless, it progressed at a very rapid pace. The government, actively involved in industrial promotion, protected infant industries and provided soft financing terms to encourage private investment. Huge oil revenues financed all sorts of government projects, created a modern infrastructure, stimulated internal demand, and paid for needed imports. As was usual at the time in many developing countries, a large number of state-owned enterprises emerged, operating in almost all sectors of economic activity.

The results were quite impressive. Not only was economic growth high, but inflation was very low. During the 1950s and 1960s, inflation averaged a meager 1.7 percent annually. Foreign investment was relatively strong, especially in oil and iron ore. The only problem was that with Venezuela's deep involvement in and dependence on the oil market, the country was vulnerable to instability in the external environment. But, to Venezuela's advantage, the world situation remained stable, and although oil prices were not very high and there were occasional rumblings about deteriorating terms of trade, the income from oil provided a substantial stable flow of fiscal and foreign earnings. There were still no major international trends disrupting flows and pumping up the price for oil. (See Table 4.1.)

But this price stability was short-lived, for the 1970s brought about new circumstances. By the middle of the decade, with the price of oil having gone from about US$2 per barrel to $14 and up, the country was receiving an inflow of foreign exchange that proved almost impossible to manage and invest wisely. The attempt to sterilize the excess oil income by investing it outside the country was not very successful, and President Pérez's statement that "we will administer abundance as if we were administering scarcity" was not supported by the actions of the state's institutional apparatus or, for that matter, those of most segments of society.

During the mid-1970s, growth remained high—at 6.8 percent—largely because of the explosion of oil prices; and inflation stayed relatively low—at 6.6 percent. The current account of the balance of payments showed a large surplus and international reserves breached the $9 billion

Table 4.2 The Oil Boom Period, 1974–1982

Average Yearly Inflation	12.4%
Average Yearly Rate of Growth	3.2%

Source: CORDIPLAN

barrier in 1976 and even exceeded $11 billion in 1981. This accumulation of reserves created all sorts of illusions and expectations that proved to be the basis for many policy mistakes. (See Table 4.2.)

Paradoxically, every oil shock played havoc with the country's expectations and fiscal discipline. Every time oil prices and, therefore, government income increased sharply and unexpectedly, public expenditures increased and new big-ticket projects were initiated. Unfortunately, when oil prices and government income came tumbling down, public expenditures and investment outlays not only did not go down but in some years were even increased. Expectations, politics, and the apparent irreversibility of investment projects proved government spending patterns incapable of following and adapting to the cycles of the oil markets.[2] Since 1970 oil revenues rose or fell by an amount that, on average, was equivalent to 6 percent of GDP. Almost naturally, foreign indebtedness was the preferred instrument utilized to cushion the macroeconomic bumps caused by this asynchronous pattern of fiscal income and outlays. The early 1980s found the country carrying more than $20 billion in debt with foreign banks. (Even after several reschedulings and renegotiations, the foreign debt reached about $30 billion in the mid-1980s.)

The recurring episodes of unexpected and massive inflows of foreign exchange brought about by the oil crisis, together with the continuous income that the oil industry guaranteed, allowed the state to live off of oil revenues at the expense of increased economic productivity, and without the long-term corrections that had become necessary. Venezuela continued with a policy of indiscriminate import-substitution industrialization at a time when it was no longer economically prudent. The use of higher tariffs and quotas, increased state intervention, price controls, and massive and indiscriminate subsidies and tax exemptions all deepened the structural inefficiencies afflicting the economy.

Whole industries that did not have the slightest possibility of making a freestanding, self-sustained, and long-term contribution to the country's economic well-being were allowed to grow and prosper through ever-increasing subsidies and barriers that assured their profitability while isolating them from international and even domestic competition. Productivity, especially in the manufacturing sectors, was poor, and, for long periods, tended to decrease every year.[3]

Venezuela's experience with import-substitution industrialization policies was not that different from that of many other developing countries. It did create an industrial base in a country that had had none, but it also created fertile conditions for major economic distortions to emerge. In fact, in the Venezuelan case, the combination of a state rich with oil and poor in efficient institutions tended to amplify both the virtues and the defects of an inward-oriented and highly protected and subsidized industrialization effort. For our purposes here, suffice it to say that the need to consolidate an incipient democratic system that for many years was a precious oddity with respect to most other countries in Latin America served to justify economic policies. While in retrospect they can be seen as having been unsound, at the time they seemed to make a lot of political sense.

Oil wealth allowed economically dubious decisions to appear viable and generally served to mask the negative consequences the policies were having. Thus, for many years the challenges of balancing political needs with economic constraints were not part of the agenda of Venezuelan politicians and government officials.[4] The intuition about economic dilemmas, which political leaders everywhere tend to develop, was stifled in Venezuela. The need for sound economic thinking was just not there, and individuals—economists and others—who insisted that more respect had to be accorded to the realities of economic life were regarded with disdain, if not outright contempt.

Not surprisingly, macroeconomic policymaking remained simple, primitive, and, in hindsight, extremely slow in adapting to changes occurring in Venezuela and abroad. Exchange rates, interest rates, fiscal policy, monetary policy, and trade and industrial policies were rigid, not well coordinated, if at all; and imbalances and distortions of all kinds were continuously accumulating without the public, politicians, or even most local economists doing much about it.[5] Industrial policy became an excuse to transfer public resources to politically chosen and privately owned "priority sectors." It was only a matter of time before this situation became unsustainable and needed corrections could no longer be postponed.

Each year, for eight continuous years from 1978 to 1985, the country's economy shrank. Thus reality started to catch up with Venezuela as GDP declined at a rate of 1 percent per year, and as the population grew at more than 2 percent each year. By 1985, real GDP was 25 percent lower than it had been just seven years earlier. In fact, the real income per capita in 1985 was almost 15 percent lower than it was in 1973, the year the country was propelled to a much higher income level thanks to the boom in oil revenues. Indeed, it was a striking example of an inverted Midas touch. The system was systematically turning gold—or oil—into poverty.

In fact, even if problems seemed to emerge everywhere, increasing poverty was the most serious of all. In 1981 the number of people living below the poverty line began to rise steadily, and it continued to do so throughout the rest of the decade. By 1989 it was estimated that about 53 percent of all Venezuelans could be categorized as living in poverty, an increase from the 32 percent estimate for 1982. Also in 1989, 22 percent of all households did not have enough income to cover the costs of the minimum daily food requirement—up from 10 percent in 1982.[6]

In the external sector, capital flight, escalation of debt owed to foreign creditors, and severance of Venezuela's access to international credit markets combined to create another first for modern Venezuelan policymakers: a severe foreign exchange shortage. Capital flight accelerated from 1978 to 1982, when internal interest rates fell below international levels and the whole structure of incentives provided strong motivations to sell the nation's currency—the bolivar—and buy foreign exchange. The incentives were not only economic. The country also witnessed the baffling scene of the president of the Central Bank exhorting Venezuelans to buy US dollars in a move that, according to his understanding of economics, would support the Bank's efforts to drain liquidity and curb inflation. The capital flight episodes of the eighties became recurrent and massive. Estimates of the foreign assets privately held by Venezuelans abroad at the end of the decade range between $50 and $80 billion. Foreign debt, which began rising in the early 1970s, increased from about $2 billion in 1973 to over $35 billion in 1982.

That year, Mexico defaulted on the service of its huge foreign debt, precipitating the debt crisis that had been brewing for some time. Among other effects, this event brought to an almost complete halt the flow of foreign funds to the entire Latin American region. Thus, by being unable to contract new foreign debt, the Venezuelan public sector lost the only instrument it had hitherto utilized to deal with external imbalances. So it had to innovate.

In 1983, the last year of the government of President Luis Herrera Campins, a Christian Democrat, restrictions and controls on foreign exchange were established in an attempt to curb a process that seriously threatened to leave the country without reserves. This exchange control regime—known by its acronym "RECADI"—became the source of major economic maladies and, as is normal with such schemes, a magnet for corruption. Essentially, the system was based on having several different prices for foreign exchange. Importers of "priority goods," ranging from medicines to automotive parts, had one exchange rate; importers of other goods and services considered of lesser priority had another. Private firms that had to service their foreign debt operated under their own exchange rate; the general public had its own, too. Each year the government estimated how much foreign exchange was available and assigned quotas to each of the different lists of sectors—and even to individual importers—according to criteria that were often changed and seldom very transparent. Jockeying for the largest possible quota of foreign currency at the lowest officially available exchange rate became the single most important objective for the Venezuelan private sector during the 1980s. It also attracted the interest of politicians, union leaders, journalists, and even media personalities and beauty queens that, through their contacts and influence on public officials, could shift the allocation of some dollars to their or their friends' companies. The opportunities to make a fast and sizeable fortune were plenty, and they were not left untapped.

Beyond the decision to impose foreign exchange controls, no other urgently needed policy changes were implemented. Interest rates were maintained at levels far below inflation and the depreciation of the parallel exchange rate. Public spending continued to be badly disoriented; mismanaged publicly owned enterprises and utilities generated large deficits and poor products and services. Servicing the foreign debt imposed large and ever-growing burdens on the balance of payments and public finances. The list of problems could go on. In this context, it was no surprise that new local and foreign private investment became a rarity, social services deteriorated, and increased economic productivity and improved income distribution generally could be found only in the speeches of politicians.

In the second half of the 1980s, a new government, Acción Democrática's president Jaime Lusinchi, continued postponing the profound policy changes that had to be made sooner or later. Like his predecessor, he attempted to deal with the deteriorating situation through partial reforms and isolated efforts. The situation, however, had not reached a sufficiently critical stage so as to prompt adoption of drastic and politically costly corrections. More profound changes were avoided even though oil prices declined sharply, in contrast with the first half of the decade when the Iran-Iraq war pushed oil prices to unprecedented heights and again generated a significant amount of revenue for the government. In 1985, the price for Venezuelan oil averaged $33 per barrel. The following year it dropped to $15 per barrel. Therefore, in 1986, government revenue from oil *declined* by 31 percent from that of the preceding year, while public spending that year *increased* by 10 percent.

If the government was having difficulties managing the economy with high oil revenues, it is easy to imagine the confusion prompted by diminished oil income. (See Figures 4.1 and 4.2.) Inertia, ignorance, and lack of a shared vision about alternative policy options, coupled with a scheme that made existing price distortions very profitable to practically all segments of the Venezuelan elite, eliminated the possibility of real

45

change from the government's agenda. Moreover, presidential elections were scheduled for December 1988, and given that any change would in the short run be highly unpopular, it became obvious to everyone that no changes would occur before the elections. Furthermore, the long-standing tradition of expanding public spending on the eve of general elections was carefully cultivated. So, even with a sharp decline in government revenues, major expansions in public spending, credit, and foreign exchange availability were allowed. To no one's surprise, in 1988 the economy grew by almost 5 percent. In contrast, the country seemed very surprised when the new government disclosed in early 1989 that foreign reserves were severely depleted, that in 1988 the country had run a fiscal deficit exceeding 9 percent of GDP, that the current account of the balance of payments had its largest deficit in history, and that all prices in the economy, from interest rates and eggs to medicines and bus fares, were artificially low and impossible to sustain.

For decades, Venezuelans had consumed more than they produced, and unavoidably, to restore balance, real incomes and consumption had to decline.

Figure 4.1. Government Petroleum Revenues (Billions of 1991 $US)

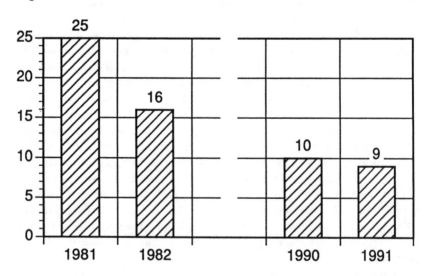

Source: CORDIPLAN

Figure 4.2. Petroleum Revenues per Capita (1991 $US)

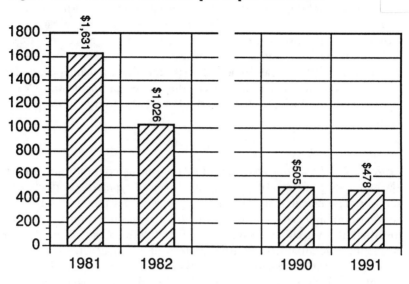

Source: CORDIPLAN

1989: Teetering on the Brink of Collapse

Elections were held on December 3, 1988. Carlos Andrés Pérez, who had already served as president between 1974 and 1979 and thus presided over the oil boom of the mid-1970s and all its accompanying economic excesses, again won the presidency. However, for the first time in many elections his political party, Acción Democrática, did not fare well. In effect, it lost its majority in both houses of Congress as well as control of many local governments. President Pérez's inauguration was held on February 2, 1989 before an unprecedented number of world leaders, a clear testament to the solid international reputation he personally enjoyed. Three weeks later, on Monday, February 27, the people of Caracas and several other major cities took to the streets.

Three days of rioting and looting left three hundred Venezuelans dead and the country overwhelmed with panic, perplexity, and rage. Not even during the most turbulent times of the 1960s, when Castroite guerrillas were operating in the country, had such a widespread and violent episode of civil disobedience and civil unrest occurred.[7] The country was discovering the hard way how the illusion of wealth and economic security had created an artificial and dangerous economic,

47

social, and institutional setting that sooner or later had to collapse. Inflation, capital flight, internal and external deficits, growing poverty, and the serious deterioration of public services were the most visible symptoms of the problems facing an economy in an extreme state of macroeconomic and institutional disarray.

In fact, as 1989 began Venezuela was indeed approaching economic collapse. There were five areas in which the deepest problems were clearly evident, and for which effective government action was urgently needed.

Five Problem Areas

Repressed inflation. First was the problem of repressed inflation. Venezuela had a long history of price controls on all types of products and services. The classic justification for them was that the lack of foreign competition imposed by the government's protectionist policies, and the insufficient internal competition associated with the small number of large and influential firms that characterized many sectors of the economy, made it impossible to rely on market-determined prices. Therefore, the ministry of industry—officially called the Ministry of Development— had among its many other duties that of officially setting the prices of an immense—and administratively overwhelming—array of products and services.[8]

But even with all the efforts directed at controlling prices, inflation averaged an unprecedented 23 percent annually from 1986 to 1988. A 93 percent devaluation of the bolivar in 1986, aimed at restoring a measure of equilibrium to the economy, also added to existing inflationary pressures. At the same time, the fact that elections were scheduled for December 1988 had two effects: (1) It made it easy for everyone, from housewives to foreign-exchange speculators, to target the first semester of 1989 as the time in which major policy changes—and therefore price hikes and devaluation—would take place; (2) Confirming general expectations, the government's reluctance to authorize price increases heightened during the last part of 1987 and grew steadily throughout 1988, when it essentially attempted a general price freeze.[9]

The combination of widespread expectations of price increases with artificially low official prices and interest rates, coupled with a "normal" (expansionary) election year fiscal policy, fueled demand at a very rapid pace. At the same time, all kinds of disincentives and bottlenecks for an adequate supply response were in place. The consequences of this explosive mixture of policies did not take long to become apparent. Plant stoppages, hoarding, the breakdown of formal distribution systems, speculation, heightened corruption, and the emergence of black market transactions for almost everything—cars, milk, bank loans, flour, hospital beds, and so forth—resulted in the most severe shortages that Venezuelans had ever experienced. Manufacturers reduced their operations to avoid losses from low prices, merchants held onto their inventories, awaiting higher prices, and consumers bought all they could before prices increased again. A country in which even the poorest citizens had been accustomed to a comparatively enviable access to basic staples and consumer goods started to face, for the first time in its modern history, Soviet-style rationing, long lines, and months of anxieties and tensions associated with not finding even the most basic staples in the grocery stores. The fact that everyone "knew" or suspected that the products were in stock somewhere, waiting for the new prices to be authorized, was an added element of frustration and anger.[10]

Balance of payments deficits. A second crisis area was the external sector. Balance-of-payments deficits, not a frequent economic trait of oil-exporting countries, started to occur, reccurring every year between 1986 and 1989. The sharp drop of oil prices in the mid-1980s, the rise of international interest rates, the need to service a $30 billion foreign debt, impaired access to the international credit markets, severely constrained nonoil exports, and the continuous lack of investor confidence, with its capital-flight consequences, were among the factors that contributed to the weakening of Venezuela's international finances. But the country's balance of payments was not only weak, but also grossly distorted. The natural trend towards an overvalued exchange rate that oil exporting countries exhibit—the "Dutch Disease" phenomenon—was greatly amplified by the nature of Venezuela's exchange-control regime and by the context in which such a system had to be administered. As noted, highly politicized economic decisionmaking, coupled with extremely poor government organization and a weak institutional setting to fine-tune its operations and curb excesses, made the foreign-exchange allocation system a major source of distortions and economic deterioration. By making foreign exchange very cheap, not only were nonoil exporting possibilities impaired, but there were also great incentives to import goods and export capital. This partly explains how in the midst of an economic crisis the country imported almost $8 billion worth of goods in 1986, $9 billion in 1987, and $12 billion in 1988. To put these figures in perspective, it is worth noting that in 1988 the imports of all countries in Latin America totalled $115.1 billion, meaning that those of Venezuela, with only 4 percent of the region's population, accounted for more than 10 percent of the imports of the entire region.

This trend pushed international reserves to critically low levels. At the end of 1988, the current account registered a $6 billion deficit and the country lost half of its net international reserves.

The Budget deficit. Third, the growth of the budget deficit was uncontrollable. Although in 1985 the fiscal budget had a surplus equal to 3 percent of GDP, by 1988 it had turned into a deficit equal to 9.4 percent of the GDP, thus becoming a major source of inflationary pressures. The sheer magnitude and complexity of the government's current expenditures, the unavoidable and growing burden of debt service payments, and the huge and growing losses of public utilities and other state-owned enterprises guaranteed large—and ever-growing—deficits.[11]

Financial controls. Fourth was the problem of financial repression. Interest rates were also administered by a government that not only kept them at artificially low levels, but also instituted all sorts of mandatory quotas to direct credit to specific "priority" sectors at even lower rates. Interest rates were fixed well below the inflation rate, so borrowing domestically to buy foreign exchange became a no-lose proposition. As we saw, the devastation of international reserves did not take long, as capital flight was further stimulated by interest rates that were low in comparison to both expected inflation and international interest rates. Real interest rates were negative by 15 percentage points in 1987 and 12.5 percentage points in 1988. As usual, the poor and the middle class bore the burden of misguided policies that had as their stated intention the protection of these same social groups. So while any savings that the poor or middle income groups might have deposited in the domestic financial system would be earning about 13 percent per year in interest—with inflation running at about double that rate—credit at the official, low interest rate, for all practical purposes, was impossible to obtain. Instead, credit was more accessible for those individuals with close links to shareholders and managers of the private banks, who had foreign exchange collaterals to offer as a guarantee for their loans, or who had the political connections needed to open the credit windows of state-owned banks. Additionally, private banks devised sophisticated schemes of special commissions and processing fees that in practice allowed them to charge a higher interest rate for their loans than what the government had determined. This made it possible for them to fund themselves at the low official rate and lend at significantly higher rates—not a bad deal.

State intervention. Finally, a solution to Venezuela's economic difficulties could not be found without addressing the structural problems created by the country's indiscriminate application of import-substitution industrialization policies and an overreliance on the state as an economic agent. These included excessive state intervention, a highly concentrated, oligopolistic industrial structure, low productivity, and significant obstacles for nonoil exports. But even more important than the resources it controlled, the state's significance stemmed from the fact that its intervention was all-encompassing, inefficient, and for the most part highly regressive in its effects on the distribution of income and wealth. With regard to trade, for example, a regime of tariff and nontariff barriers—including mandatory permits for 80 percent of all imports and as much as 940 percent import duties on some products— ensured that Venezuela's industry would be protected against more efficient international competition. It also ensured that growth of the nonoil export sector was further stunted because tariffs increased the prices of imported raw materials, thus making it very difficult for a Venezuelan firm to compete internationally, given that it had to pay more than its competitors for the same inputs. Exporters also had to deal with ports that were extremely costly to use and highly unreliable, with an inefficient state-owned shipping company that imposed all sorts of constraints and increased transport costs, and with power, water, and telecommunications services that, while cheap, were also severely plagued by stoppages, inefficiencies, and extremely low quality. In many sectors, industrial firms were also obliged to buy their inputs from state-owned monopolies—in iron, steel, aluminum, chemicals, petrochemicals, and so forth—that did not often meet adequate standards of quality and that usually required burdensome bureaucratic procedures in order to obtain them.

All of this, of course, affected not only exporters but the economy as a whole. Together with the macroeconomic problems, these structural problems generated the forces underlying the trend toward declining productivity that the country exhibited for so many years. It also helps explain why, for example, in 1989 the country had the same number of industrial establishments as it had a decade earlier—about 10,000—and why, after having been one of the most attractive sites for foreign investment in the region, Venezuela had become one of countries with the lowest flow of inward direct investment in South America. (In the 1990s, Bolivia was the only country in the Andean region, which is not very dynamic, that attracted less foreign investment than did Venezuela.) Economic mismanagement was also a central reason why, during the "lost decade" of the 1980s, when per capita GDP in Latin America dropped an average of 9.4 percent, Venezuela's per capita GDP dropped 20 percent.

In sum, at the start of 1989, Venezuela was in obvious economic danger, operating with a grossly and increasingly isolated and inefficient economy, and on the verge of a prolonged period of hyperinflation and even more rapid socioeconomic decline. The clearest indicator of the tremendous challenge facing the country, and the most ominous sign for its future, was the continuing rise in poverty. By 1988, the number of households living below the poverty line had increased to approximately 600,000 (a tenfold increase since 1981), the real per capita income was equal to what it had been in 1973, and the infant mortality rate was double the rates in countries like Jamaica and Costa Rica that had just half of Venezuela's per capita income.

Something had to be done, and partial and halfhearted reforms like those attempted in the recent past would not do.

"El Gran Viraje"—The Great Turnaround

The Pérez government called its policy package "The Great Turn-around." People in the streets called it *El Paquete*—The Package—a Venezuelan popular expression used to indicate a problematic, cumbersome situation. Both names were accurate.

Not many had anticipated that *El Viraje* was going to be that steep or that *El Paquete* was going to be that problematic. The new policy orientation was indeed a radical—and surprising—departure from the past.

While insisting during the 1988 electoral campaign that profound changes were needed and that, if elected, he was going to implement them, Pérez was always very careful not to give too many details about the general policies that he had in mind to "modernize the economy." Given the orientation of his previous presidency, the nature of his party's attitudes, and the success with which local elites had historically fought attempts at curbing their privileges, Pérez's statements were taken more as electoral rhetoric than as the deep personal commitment they turned out to be.

As president, Pérez showed by his actions that he was truly determined to do whatever was needed, not only to avoid the major threats that the economy was facing in 1989, but also to deal with the deeply rooted causes of the country's long-term economic and social deterioration. His actions also showed that he was convinced that he had no better option than to pursue economic policies not completely dependent for their success on the existence of a state capable of effective independent action. In fact, profound disillusionment with the possibilities of state action in a developing country, more than trust in the workings of the free market, seemed to be the underlying thrust of his current economic thinking.[12] Furthermore, Pérez exhibited an unusual disposition to incur all the political costs inevitably associated with reforms like the ones his government was undertaking. This willingness was obviously based on his belief that these short-term political costs would be more than compensated for by the historical recognition that he had been the leader responsible for taking the country off the declining path onto which it had fallen.

The first sign that Pérez was willing to go beyond vague promises came with the appointment of his key ministers. To the surprise of everyone, including some of the appointees themselves, the new president brought to his cabinet a group of relatively young, foreign-trained, politically inexperienced professionals with no party affiliations. They tended to be either academics or respected professional managers in the private sector and, for most of them, it was their first public sector job. This was a sharp departure from the established practice of having political activists occupying the main government jobs.[13]

While the set of policies adopted by the Pérez government implied a radical and even revolutionary break with the immediate past, they had virtually the same general goals, assumptions, and design of most other reform programs adopted in the late 1980s and early 1990s in Latin America, and, for that matter, throughout the world. Of course, there were special traits of the Venezuelan program, but it was not that different in its basic design from what has been referred to as the "Washington Consensus" developed and promoted by the multilateral financial institutions and some think tanks.[14] Macroeconomic stabilization, trade liberalization, deregulation, and privatization were the building blocks on which reform efforts had to be based.

Following this orientation, the initial phase of the Venezuelan program was aimed at restoring macroeconomic stability and eliminating price distortions. It was based on a set of measures including the establishment of a single, freely floating exchange rate, the removal of price controls on all private goods and services except those on a list of eighteen specific staple items, market-determined interest rates, reductions in real public spending, and significant increases in the prices of goods produced by the public sector as well as in the rates of public utilities. Complete overhaul of the tax system, including the adoption of a value-added tax, was to be implemented to ensure that government revenues would no longer be so inordinately dependent on the taxes levied on the oil industry.

Fiscal and monetary expansion were to be prudently administered. Another goal was the negotiated reduction of the foreign debt burden on the country's finances, together with the restoration of normal relations with foreign creditors and the international financial community at large.

Macroeconomic stabilization measures were to be complemented by major structural reforms. Trade liberalization; capital goods and labor markets deregulation; reform of the agricultural, industrial, and financial sectors; foreign investment promotion; and an ambitious privatization program were the main components of the structural reform package. Additionally, the traditional approach of governmental policies aimed at helping the poor, based on generalized and inefficient price subsidies, were to be abandoned in favor of more focused efforts directly targeting the most vulnerable groups of society. The government also devised social "safety nets" designed to provide financial, nutritional, and health assistance to those more severely affected by the inevitable hardships imposed by the situation. Furthermore, the Pérez administration announced state and political reforms, along with public sector restructuring and general institutional modernization, as part of its goals.

It was hard to believe that all of the elements of the Pérez plan could be achieved or even adequately addressed. Indeed, few found the plan credible at all.

Turning It Around: Surprise, Surprise

The government acted with dazzling speed. The administration eliminated exchange controls and established the free convertibility of the bolivar, which immediately produced a 170 percent devaluation. It freed interest rates, which climbed from 13 percent to more than 40 percent per year, liberalized virtually all prices, and increased the rates of electricity, water, telephones, gasoline, public transportation, and most other public services.[15]

The Pérez administration proceeded to remove nontariff barriers covering 94 percent of local manufactures and eliminate special permits for exports, simultaneously restructuring the tariff system, thus bringing the country's average tariff level down from 35 percent in 1988 to around 10 percent in 1990. Yearly tariff reduction rounds were scheduled and rigorously implemented which, together with the country's entry into GATT, generated the freest trade regime in Venezuela's recent history. The authorities also secured the financial assistance of the International Monetary Fund, the World Bank, and the Inter-American Development Bank.

At the same time, the government started an intensive round of negotiations with foreign commercial banks aimed at reducing and restructuring the country's $19.5 billion public debt. These negotiations eventually led to an agreement that changed the composition of the debt, lowered annual interest payments, and secured a seven-year grace period for the payment of principal.[16] (See Figure 4.3.)

By early 1990 a new foreign investment regime was in place, eliminating almost all restrictions on foreign investors and minimizing government interference in their financial, commercial, and technological transactions. Government prescreening or preapproval of foreign investment projects was no longer required, all restrictions on profit remittances and capital repatriation were lifted, and, for the first time, the stock market was opened to foreign investors. Pérez's team introduced new legislation in Congress to create a completely altered income tax system and a value-added tax, and the government took concrete steps

Figure 4.3. External Debt Service, 1988-1991 (Percentage of exports of goods and services)

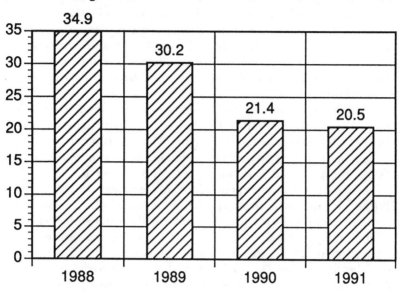

Source: CORDIPLAN

to privatize state-owned enterprises. In fact, by 1991 four commercial banks, the national airline, the phone company, as well as the cellular telephone system, a shipyard, the ports, sugar mills, and several hotels, had all been privatized.

At the end of that year, a specific schedule for the transfer of controlling state equity to the private sector was announced. It included the privatization of sugar mills, hotels, several horse-racing tracks, another airline, the Caracas water supply system, the regional power distribution facilities, the public television network, and many other enterprises and utilities. This meant one or more privatizations *per month.* It was hard to believe that not much time had passed since one former president had explained that the phone company could never be sold for national security reasons, another had ridiculed the proposal to privatize the airline by equating it to a plan to sell the national flag, and a third had theorized publicly about the impossibility of selling any utility on the grounds that it would be impossible to find private buyers.

Social policies were effectively changed and new social programs initiated. Indirect subsidies, in which payments and other transfers were made to specific private firms producing basic staples in order to keep their prices low—such as corn flour, milk, sugar, poultry, sardines, and so forth—were eliminated. Instead, a massive nutritional grant program

(Beca Alimentaria, or "Food Grant"), which established a direct cash transfer to mothers of children enrolled in schools located in poor urban and rural areas, was initiated along with a maternal-child health program to provide free medical and nutritional assistance to pregnant and nursing women and small children. Also, the government created a worker protection plan based on unemployment compensation payments for six months as well as several other support mechanisms for aiding laid-off workers.

Changes in the central government were initiated and some ministries implemented major reforms in their structure and in the traditional ways in which they conducted their affairs. The government also submitted a new law to Congress containing significant reforms in the existing division of responsibilities within the central government.

President Pérez also became a force in December 1989 in favor of political reforms, catalyzing and orienting change—which brought the first direct election of state governors (who had previously been personally appointed by the president)—as well as to the creation of a new directly elected official, the city mayor. A fierce national debate also began, leading to the eventual approval of an amendment adopting uninominal and direct elections for members of Congress, as opposed to the then-existing system of voting for party-determined lists.

This meant that 1989 was not only a year of profound changes in economic policies and living conditions; it was also a year in which unprecedented political transformations took place. No society can easily digest and process so many important and varied changes occurring almost simultaneously. Societal change on such a broad scale, almost by definition, is disjointed, traumatic, and extremely difficult to manage well, if it can be managed at all. The Venezuelan experience confirms this.

The Shocking Consequences of Turning It Around

In just one month—March 1989—Venezuelans experienced almost as much inflation (21 percent) as they had usually had over an entire year. Even though during the following months the pace of price increases diminished significantly, in 1989 yearly inflation still reached more than 80 percent, the highest ever. Prices had not only to catch up with almost two years of artificial repression, but also had to account for the major cost increases associated with new higher prices for money, foreign currency, utilities, raw materials, intermediate products, and all services, from insurance policies to transportation fees.

The 1989 budget was reduced by 10 percent in real terms and the public sector deficit declined from 9.3 percent of GDP a year earlier to 1.3 percent. The economy shrank by almost 10 percent (GDP fell by 8.6 percent in real terms and nonoil GDP contracted by 9.8 percent). The impact of all this was substantial impoverishment. Unemployment rose from about 7 percent in 1988 to almost 10 percent at the end of 1989, while disposable personal income, which had already declined by about 2 percent the year before, shrank by an overwhelming 14 percent in 1989.[17] Real salaries declined by a further 11 percent in 1989, thus bringing the decline over the decade to 45 percent.[18]

The social and political upheavals of the period were to be expected. The country witnessed periodic strikes and public demonstrations by teachers, hospital workers, university professors, students, farmers, drugstore owners, police officials, home mortgage holders, public sector workers, and a variety of other interest groups protesting the severe impact government actions were having in worsening their economic plight.

Interestingly, however, although the social and political situation became extremely tense and the frequency and stridency of the protests were a cause for concern, major new episodes of generalized riots or even violent clashes between police and the groups participating in the marches failed to materialize. One possible explanation for this is that the early, massive outburst of violence had so scared all segments of society that no one wanted to run the risk of being held responsible for any new bout of generalized violence.[19] The fact that the events of February 1989 started with relatively minor incidents and rapidly escalated to massive, spontaneous rioting seem to have produced a sobering dose of caution and self-restraint among organizers of strikes and public marches. It can be speculated that if such an early and highly traumatic event that affected large segments of society in one way or another had not taken place, a series of intermittent, more localized episodes of public violence might have occurred throughout 1989 and even 1990.

In fact, perhaps one of the most noticeable features of the first three years of the Venezuelan reforms was the relative lack of organized, politically motivated social violence to accompany the sweeping changes, imposed on a society either far from enthusiastic or not widely convinced of the appropriateness of such changes. On the other hand, the explosive increase in street crimes, muggings, and violent home robberies was a concomitant and tragic trend of hitherto unexamined sociopolitical effects. The manifest incompetence of the police in dealing with a situation that clearly transcended their capacity and resources, and the ineffectiveness of the judicial system, led to a situation of virtual impunity that nearly eliminated the risks of committing property crimes. Inflation, unemployment, the collapse of social services, and the general increase in poverty created the incentive for many to seek through crime what had become very difficult to obtain legally. Thus, Venezuela's main cities became "normal" Latin American cities in the sad sense that personal safety was a luxury only a few could afford.

On the social and political fronts, the changes brought about by the

Great Turnaround were difficult to digest. On the macroeconomic front, however, positive results did not take long to became evident.

After the 10 percent drop in output that the country experienced in 1989, economic growth resumed at a very rapid pace. Unemployment fell from 9.6 percent in 1988 to 7.5 percent in 1991. (See Figure 4.4.) GDP grew by 5.3 percent in 1990 and by 9.2 percent in 1991, the highest rate the Venezuelan economy had experienced in thirty-five years. In these two years Venezuela had one of the fastest-growing economies in all of Latin America. (See Table 4.3 and Figure 4.5.)

While, again, oil prices and external factors—such as the Gulf War— were crucial in determining the fortunes of the Venezuelan economy, the impact of these factors was not as massive as on previous occasions and they were much shorter in duration. Furthermore, the nonoil sources of this growth, the policy framework within which it took place, and the general expectations surrounding it, were quite different from those of the past. While obviously the economy is now and will remain heavily dependent on oil, it is equally obvious that the policies adopted in 1989 have unleashed a process that over the long run may generate other sources of economic growth. Nonoil exports, for example, increased 49 percent in 1989 and 15 percent in 1990. In 1991, a sharp drop in the international price of aluminum, which accounts for a substantial

Figure 4.4. Unemployment, 1988-1991 (Percentage of labor force)

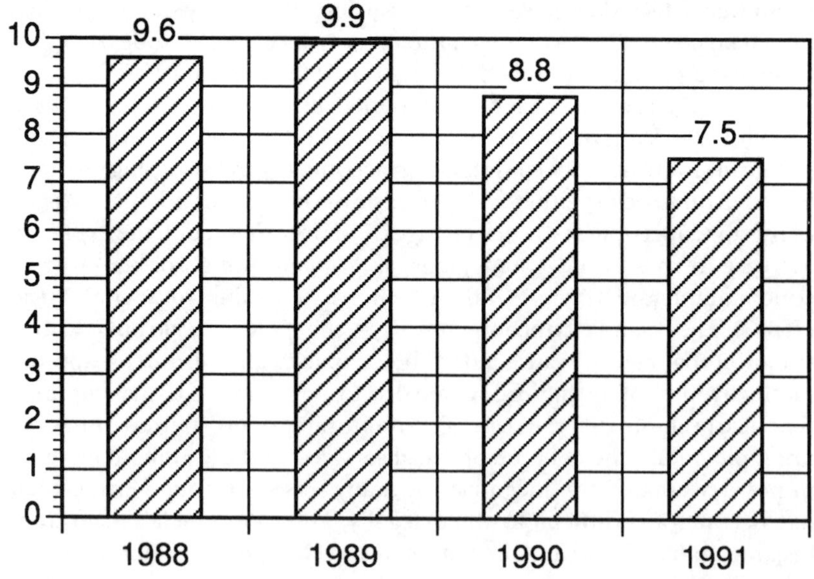

Source: CORDIPLAN

Table 4.3   The Post–Oil Boom Period (1983–1991)

		Average Yearly Inflation	Average Yearly Rate of Growth
1983–1985	Adjustment Without Structural Change	10.0	-2.3
1986–1988	Deficit-Financed Growth	23.0	5.3
1989–1991	Adjustment and Structural Change	53.1	2.1

Source: CORDIPLAN

share of nonoil exports, led these to decline. (See Figure 4.6.)

Perhaps the more important point to note is that private sector exports are rapidly showing signs of great vitality and potential, having grown by 78 percent and 26 percent respectively during those two years.[20] Although such extremely high growth was due to special nonrecurring circumstances and therefore could not be sustained in the short run, there is no reason to believe that Venezuelan private firms will not continue to expand significantly in the international market. (See Figure 4.7.)

Figure 4.5. Growth of GDP (Percentage)

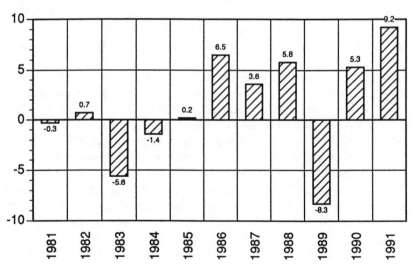

Source: CORDIPLAN

Figure 4.6. Non-Oil Exports, 1986-1991 (Billions of $US)

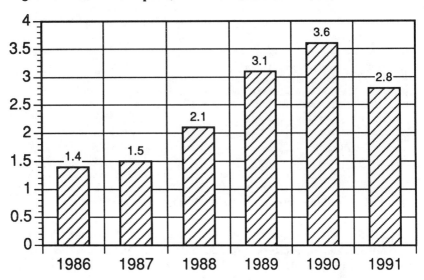

Source: CORDIPLAN

New private industrial investment, stagnant for most of the previous decade, is also showing strong signs of revitalization. In particular, export-oriented, resource-based private foreign investment is bound to account for a much larger share of Venezuelan exports in the future. It is useful to note, for perspective, that the book value of the total existing stock of foreign direct investment in the country at the end of 1990 was about $3.6 billion and that conservative estimates indicate that inflows of foreign investment could exceed $10 billion during the 1990s.[21] The privatization of 40 percent of the phone company in late 1991 brought in $1.9 billion and its planned expansion is expected to generate about $1 billion annually in additional investment in the coming years.

Interesting though partial evidence of the renewed investor confidence in Venezuela is the unprecedented boom in prices in the Caracas stock market. In 1990, no other stock market *in the world* had a better performance in real dollar terms.[22] In 1991, the boom tended to level off—growth was 34 percent in US dollars—but it continued to show signs of a clear trend that is very different from those of the past. The same can be said about market prices for Venezuelan debt. While in February 1989 an investor could buy one dollar of Venezuelan debt for 27 cents, in 1991 the same investor would have had to pay about 70 cents. Furthermore, at the end of 1991 both the government and private

Figure 4.7. Total Exports and Imports, 1981–1991 (Billions of $US)

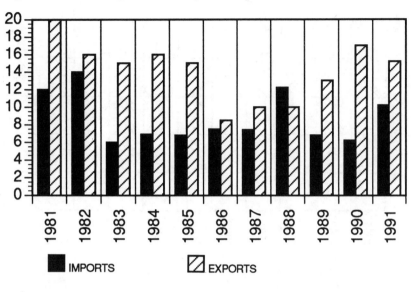

■ IMPORTS   ▨ EXPORTS

Source: CORDIPLAN

Venezuelan corporations could claim great success at placing new debt instruments in international financial markets, an event that few would have thought possible one or two years earlier.

The debt renegotiation, the temporary increase in oil prices, the expansion of nonoil exports, the revitalization of investor confidence, the ensuing reversal of the trend toward capital flight, new flows of foreign direct investment, and the moderate increase in imports during the program's first two years, all generated a strong balance-of-payments position. (See Figure 4.8.) The current account moved from a $6 billion deficit in 1988 to surpluses of more than $2 billion in 1989, $8 billion in 1990, and $2.6 billion in 1991.[23] All this allowed the country's gross international reserves to almost double during that period.

Closely related to these trends, of course, is the foreign exchange regime. In principle, under the regime adopted in 1989 the rate is "freely" determined by the supply and demand of foreign exchange, but the fact is that in Venezuela the main supplier of foreign exchange to the market is the state, given that it owns the oil company, the country's largest producer of hard currency. Every day the Central Bank sells in the market an amount of foreign exchange that is a function of the day's demand, the availability of other suppliers, and its reserve accumulation targets. Given the constraints imposed by the Central Bank's reserve

Figure 4.8. Balance of Payments, 1981-1991 (Billions of $US)

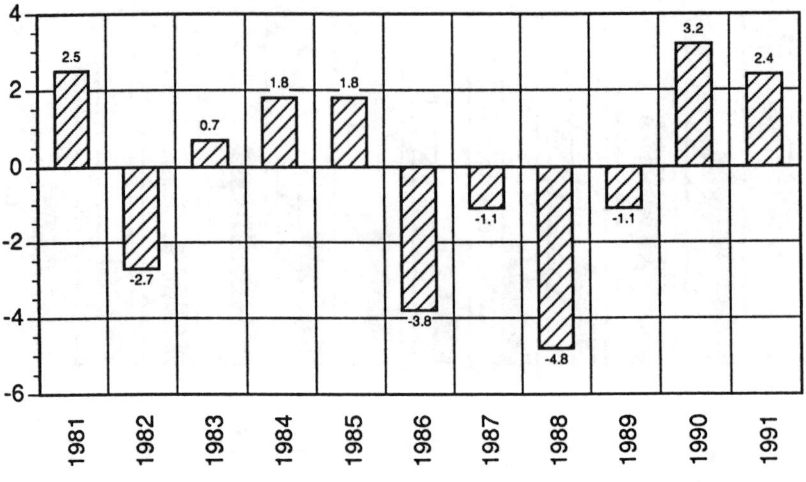

Source: CORDIPLAN

targets, when the demand for reserves far exceeds the available supply, the bolivar experiences a minidevaluation. This system has generated a great deal of political and theoretical controversy.[24] However, it has also achieved in practice the lowest currency volatility since the fixed exchange rate system collapsed in 1983. After the initial devaluation in 1989, the currency has been sliding rather smoothly and without the major upheavals in the exchange rate that had characterized the period during which exchange controls were in place.[25] Although exporters complain that the exchange rate is overvalued and, therefore, does not provide them with a sufficient margin to compete internationally, some economists have argued that the rate is undervalued and does not provide the economy with a strong enough "anchor" to hold down the imported component of domestic inflation.[26] Be that as it may, the fact is that the end result of the first three years has been one of enviable currency stability and the avoidance of gross distortion either in the price or the allocation of foreign exchange.

The results of the fiscal and monetary policies are not as easy to ascertain; they experienced wide swings in the first three years of the program. While in 1989 the government was able to achieve a solid fiscal stance, the pace of progress in the following years tended to lag significantly behind advances in other economic and institutional areas. (See

Figure 4.9. Non-Oil Current Fiscal Income (Billions of 1991 $US)

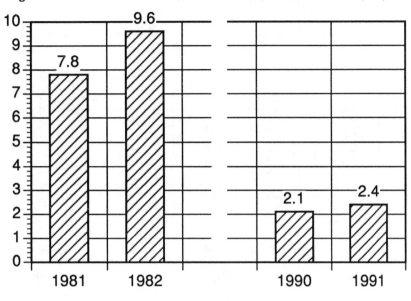

Source: CORDIPLAN

Figure 4.9.) Delays in securing congressional approval of crucial laws to increase public revenues and rationalize public spending, in implementing institutional changes in the Finance Ministry—such as customs reform, tax collection, budget construction and execution, financial sector supervision, treasury management, and so forth—and in periodically adjusting the initial price increases for public sector goods—such as gasoline, fertilizers, electricity—greatly contributed to the curbing of progress in this area.

Furthermore, the rigidity of current expenditures and the legal framework regulating their definition and disbursement, coupled with the fact that the Gulf War spurred high expectations about the level of fiscal revenues, made it even more difficult for a government that lacked the support of even its own party in Congress to impose a greater level of austerity in its public finances.[27] The fact of the matter is that even if major efforts were made at restraining public spending, a combination of political pressures, institutional deficiencies, unanticipated and uncontrollable external events, and sheer bureaucratic inertia conspired against more sound fiscal management. However, the fiscal situation never got out of hand; in fact, the country showed a deficit of 1 percent of GDP in the consolidated public sector in 1989, a small surplus in 1990, and, thanks to the income derived from privatization, a surplus of 1.3

Figure 4.10. Public Sector Balance, 1986-1991 (As percentage of GDP)

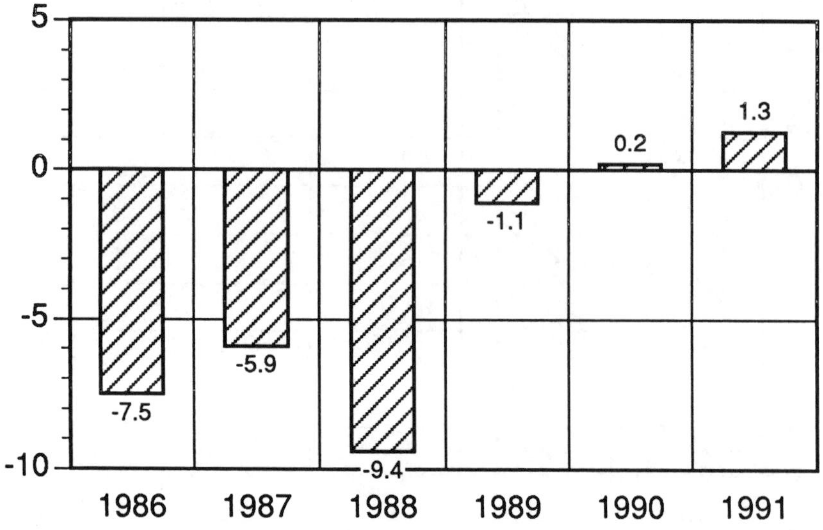

Source: CORDIPLAN

percent of GDP in 1991. (See Figure 4.10.) These were, of course, not bad indicators at all, given that the country had only recently posted a deficit of more than 9 percent of GDP in its fiscal account. Nonetheless, these aggregates masked a much more complex and confusing reality in which the end results were more a function of unplanned events than of the fine-tuned management of public finances. The fact that the fiscal aggregates did not show an alarming picture also had the effect of removing from the government's list of urgent priorities the systematic restructuring of public spending and the Ministry of Finance. The chronic and profound fiscal crisis of the Venezuelan state did not get the attention that it deserved from the government as a whole, from Congress, or from the general public.

A certain degree of complacency caused by the initial positive results, together with insufficient information about the fiscal reality and the unavoidable emergence of "adjustment fatigue," set the stage for continuing delays in securing a more robust fiscal stance. Very probably these delays, if not eliminated, will be the source of some degree of economic instability in the future.

In order to compensate for the rapid increase in public spending in 1990, the government initiated a highly restrictive monetary policy that naturally caused interest rates to skyrocket and remain, in nominal terms,

Figure 4.11. Inflation, 1981-1991 (Percentage change in CPI)

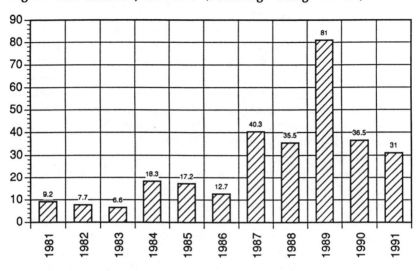

Source: CORDIPLAN

at fairly high levels. High, generally positive, real interest rates and systematic efforts at draining liquidity through open market operations were the primary tools used to counter the deleterious effects of public spending (due to both its nature and high level) on the exchange rate and inflation.

In fact, although inflation fell sharply from its 81 percent level in 1989, dropping to 36.5 percent in 1990 and about 31 percent in 1991, it remains high. (See Figure 4.11.) The many different hypotheses advanced to explain the slow rate of price decline share two factors that seem to carry particular weight. The first is the absence of better coordination of fiscal and monetary policy. The second involves the persistence of oligopolistic pricing practices in several major industrial sectors. It is usually assumed that the lowering of tariff barriers and liberalization of imports will tend to curb the pricing excesses of the highly concentrated local firms; this clearly was not the case in the initial stage of the Venezuelan experience. Many years of import substitution and promotion of manufacturing operations, coupled with price controls at the end stages of distribution channels, stifled the development of an independent retail and distribution sector and generated great incentives for subsidized manufacturers to develop their own marketing and distribution networks. It is through these highly oligopolistic, manufacturer-controlled channels that the new imports provided by a more liberal trade regime had to be distributed.

In practice, in some industrial sectors local manufacturers rapidly "reconverted"—they became importers and utilized the same marketing channels and pricing practices they had been using all along. This tended to occur most often in the sectors that had enjoyed the most protection and were, therefore, the most vulnerable to the competition of imports. They were also the more oligopolistic in their structure and behavior. Food, automotive parts, cars, medicines, appliances, textiles, paper, packaging and printing products, and electrical and construction materials were all good examples of a pattern that led to increases in the overall consumer price index that were double those of the wholesale price index.[28]

In theory, over time new competitors and new distribution companies will erode the market power of existing firms, thus bringing about more intense price competition. But in practice, the entry of new competitors in the domestic distribution and retail sector will greatly depend on the existence of a business climate that makes investment, other than the export-oriented, resource-based variety, attractive. As Selowsky[29] has indicated in his characterization of the evolution of the adjustment process, the sustained activation of private investment is the last stage to occur and it usually takes a rather long time. If the Venezuelan case is typical, then it is important to revise the usual assumptions that led economists and policymakers to believe that trade liberalization is bound to have a substantial impact on domestic competition in the initial stages of a structural reform process. Note that the more significant these oligopolistic rigidities become in inhibiting price competition and holding inflation at a lower level, the longer it takes for the stabilization efforts to have their beneficial effects. This in turn impairs the business climate and may eventually even cause postponement of the sort of private investment that could help to administer a healthier dose of price competition in the economy.

But the inflation rate's resistance to a faster decline or the difficulty in gaining firmer ground for the country's fiscal stance were not the only aspects that presented a stark contrast with the rapid and positive results observed in economic growth, the reestablishment of fundamental macroeconomic equilibria, privatization, and the attraction of the interest of the international investment community. The results of efforts aimed at improving the social situation of the lower and middle classes also lagged dramatically behind needs and expectations.

Before the reforms, the country mainly relied on generalized food subsidies and price controls to cushion the poor from adverse economic conditions. The problem was that only 40 percent of the subsidized goods were consumed by the poor while the rest were consumed by the middle and higher income groups and by industry or were exported by "creative entrepreneurs."[30] Directly targeted efforts to channel social goods and services to specific vulnerable groups were often utilized by the party in power as instruments of political clientelism and to build electoral support. This pattern greatly distorted the functioning of the institutions in charge of delivering social services and, together with their capture by their unions, made them highly corrupt and inefficient. This helps to explain why, even though Venezuela consistently spent about 40 percent of its budget and 10 to 14 percent of GDP on the social sectors in the 1970s and even though it had the highest per capita social expenditure in Latin America, its poverty indicators are worse than those of much poorer countries.[31]

The elimination of subsidies and price controls in 1989, the reduction in real terms of the public sector budget, and the increase in unemployment created a very difficult situation. The new social programs that directly targeted the poor were established and put into operation, and by 1990 almost 1 percent more of GDP per year was devoted to them. The government implemented a program of small, labor-intensive infrastructure projects designed to alleviate unemployment. The critical problem, however, was not one of high unemployment or lack of financial resources for the social sectors. Rather, it was that the previous policies had masked the fact that all social service delivery systems had in fact collapsed or were performing at minimum capacity. The Health and Education ministries as well as the agencies in charge of providing housing, nutritional support, and maternal and child care to the poor had been barely functioning despite the massive infusion of budget funding. As operating costs were pushed up by inflation and the demand for their services grew as a consequence of the crisis, the institutional capacity that was left was further eroded and in some cases disappeared altogether. Public hospitals, for example, did not have reliable controls to avoid the periodic disappearance of materials and medical equipment, and every couple of years had to be completely reequipped, from beds to X-ray machines. Inventory management and controls were—and still are—primitive or nonexistent, and the standard practice to guarantee a minimum availability of necessary medicines was to massively overstock their warehouses, thus making the apparent consumption per capita of some medicines among the highest in the world. Attempts at correcting these problems were routinely and effectively resisted by the politically controlled medical and paramedical unions that held the government hostage to their proven capacity to paralyze the public health system, by the vested interests that extract huge profits from the highly corrupt procurement system, by the lack of trained managers capable of running a modern hospital, and by the incapacity of the state to attract and retain the few trained managers

Figure 4.12. Investment in Public Services, 1982-1991 (Billions of bolivars, 1984 = 100)

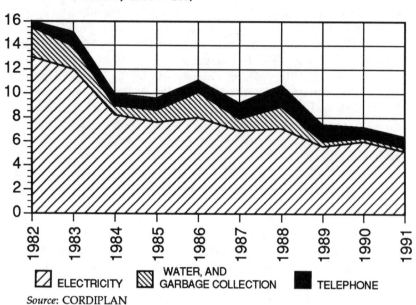

Source: CORDIPLAN

available in Venezuela. Under these circumstances, it should come as no surprise that most patients, regardless of their medical or socioeconomic condition, could be treated only after they were able to privately procure their own medical supplies, or that the vaccination coverage in the country is half the average of Latin America while its per capita expenditure on health is the second-highest in the region.

With small variations, the basic elements of this situation—congestion, waste, corruption, mismanagement, politicization, regressiveness, lack of trained personnel, and misguided unionism—could be found in almost all social delivery institutions.

The lack of a reliable social safety net, the institutional devastation of the public organizations in charge of providing social services, the severe deterioration of the efficiency of public utilities and services like water, sanitation, telephone, electricity, transportation, and the police, together with persistent price increases insufficiently matched by wage adjustments, are stark realities for very large segments of society. (See Figure 4.12.) Compared to such imminent problems, success in the balance of payments and economic growth are no more than remote abstractions.

Although these social problems accumulated over several decades and their alleviation is bound to take a long time, the fact is that

Venezuelans had expected that the sacrifices required to correct the country's problems were going to be rapidly compensated by an improvement in their living standards. In all probability, the standard of living would have declined even further in the absence of corrective actions. But, again, from the public's point of view, this is another counterfactual abstraction for which the extremely slow progress in the institutional reconstruction of public social services achieved in the first years of the reform program is certainly not a satisfactory answer. This reality is bound to have significant political repercussions. We discuss them below.

Lessons and Unanswered Questions

Three years is too little time to allow for very firm conclusions about the results of the Venezuelan reforms. Nonetheless, elements of their launching process and initial results do shed some empirical light on the assumptions and beliefs guiding the design and execution of programs having essentially the same outline. Also, even if great caution should be exerted when drawing general implications from a single case study, there are indeed some lessons from this experience that might well have more general applicability.

Implementing Change: The Pace of Reforms

The reform program reduced major macroeconomic imbalances in less than a year. Three main factors account for this speedy stabilization: (1) the oil-based potential to overcome external financing constraints; (2) the "decree driven" nature of the initial changes; and, (3) the practical impossibility of "gradualism."

While the country's external position as reflected in its balance-of-payments problems was severely damaged, its capacity to generate significant amounts of foreign exchange was never impaired. Together with the reforms, this proven export capacity generated a creditworthiness that allowed for quick debt renegotiation and the rapid recovery of Venezuela's image in international financial circles. Furthermore, in Venezuela, given that a devaluation enables the foreign exchange produced by the state oil company to generate more government revenue in local currency (which tends to be greater than government outlays of foreign exchange), a devaluation has a net positive effect on fiscal accounts. Thus, the lifting of exchange controls and the concomitant devaluation not only corrected the exchange rate distortion, but also boosted the effort to reduce the fiscal deficit. The main point to note is that in contrast to the experience of many other countries,[32] the Venezuelan adjustment was not overly constrained by the external environment.

The second factor is that government actions required to launch the adjustment process and restore macroeconomic equilibria only necessitated the stroke of a pen for their execution. All that was needed to eliminate foreign exchange controls and allow the currency to float, and to free prices and interest rates, was a cabinet meeting and the printing of a presidential decree. To a lesser extent, the same can be said about the elimination of import quotas and the lowering of tariffs. No complex organizational changes, lengthy congressional negotiations, or burdensome legislative maneuvering was needed to implement the fundamental reforms that defined the new macroeconomic framework and laid the foundations for facilitating the more institutionally complex structural changes.

All of this was possible, of course, because of the willingness of the president and the government to absorb the major political costs that these "stroke of the pen" decisions were bound to have. That no other credible options were convincingly offered at the time also helped.[33] In fact, one of the interesting lessons of the Venezuelan experience was that, though the debate over gradualism versus shock treatment in policy reform was raging in the media and professional circles both at home and abroad, it really did not present a major dilemma for the government. It soon became obvious that in order to adopt a gradualistic approach to the correction of macroeconomic distortions, a state apparatus with the ability to fine-tune macroeconomic policies and manage incremental change was required. In Venezuela, none of the institutional and organizational elements characteristic of such a state had survived the abuse of more than a decade of excess in their utilization. For example, even if the elimination of price controls was an element of the program from the beginning, their almost complete elimination in a onetime decision was not determined by a deeply ingrained and widely shared ideological belief about shock therapy. It was, instead, because the administrative system on which they were based had collapsed and the government had to react rapidly to the major supply disruptions that were taking place. The same was true of controls on foreign exchange, interest rates, and the financial sector in general.

Once the decisions were made to float the exchange rate and allow the free convertibility of the currency, the need to have real positive interest rates became imperative. Otherwise, the incentives to borrow locally at below-market interest rates to buy foreign exchange would again be created, together with an unbearable burden on the exchange rate. Additionally, if the task of defining the official, controlled prices for goods and services had become overwhelming with fixed exchange and interest rates, carrying it on with a floating currency and fluctuating interest rates became impractical. And finally, if prices were to be freed, imports also had to be liberalized in order to inject competitive pressures into local markets. This line of reasoning, the absence of reliable public institutions that made gradualism possible, the collapse of existing controls, and a government that perceived these realities and was willing to face the political consequences of corrective action, help explain how the rapid transition from one macroeconomic policy set to another—which in this case contributed to rapid stabilization—was achieved.

Overcoming Resistance to Change: Sorting Paper Tigers from Minotaurs

High inflation, perceived as the consequence of the elimination of price controls, hit the population hard. The private sector felt that trade liberalization was a mortal blow to industry. Unions feared the effects of privatization and politicians of all parties did not much like the idea of the free market, much less the virtual elimination of practices that provided the public bureaucracy, which they controlled, with the privilege of giving or withholding the myriad favors that people require of a government-controlled economy. So how could the changes be implemented?

One of the elements that made change possible was the general belief that the set of economic policies that had prevailed in the past was impossible to maintain. The experience of the 1980s, of failed attempts by two different governments to repair the existing scheme and thus avoid radical change, was an important factor in convincing some influential circles that more profound changes were needed. Additionally, the international demonstration effect of the changes in Eastern Europe and the Soviet Union, the impressive economic performance of the four Asian "dragons" and, closer to home, the results of the Chilean and Mexican reforms, greatly muted the voices calling for the maintenance of some variation of the previous regime. The almost daily airing in the highly adversarial and strident Venezuelan media of all sorts of scandals associated with the corrupt handling of the economy, especially the exchange control system, also created fertile ground for change.

Deep frustration and dissatisfaction with previous policies did not mean, however, the automatic acceptance of a market-oriented, private sector–based economic model. People knew that the system the country had was no longer acceptable—but they did not know what to replace it with.[34]

The fact that the government had an alternative, new, technically sound strategy, which it forcefully defended and swiftly implemented even in the face of massive riots during its initial stages, was crucial in avoiding the strong and possibly paralyzing opposition that the changes were destined to create. But speed, strategy, and resolve were not the only advantages the government enjoyed. The potential sources of organized opposition, namely the political parties—including the government's own, unions, and the private sector, were not only caught off guard without alternative strategies to offer, but were also weakened by opinion polls, all of which showed a drastic drop in their public credibility, and by the deterioration of their own formal institutional arrangements, which hampered their ability to react. Political parties, unions, and the private sector representative organizations (chambers, federations, and so forth) had gradually evolved into mechanisms to extract rents from the state, largely for the benefit of their leadership, though not necessarily of their constituency. This often occurred with the complicity and active participation of the government, and in some agencies the differences between the state and these actors was blurred or even nonexistent, as was the case, for example, with the unions and the Labor Ministry. By concentrating on this rent-seeking function, other tasks inimical to their institutional mission were gradually abandoned. The capacity of these sectors to base their demands on universal, informed, and well-grounded arguments was minimal, having been replaced by highly personal and clientelistic exchanges with civil servants. For example, it was very confusing for private sector representatives to switch their meetings with government officials from the elegant homes and restaurants, where specific cases were discussed and eventually resolved, to the decaying conference rooms of the ministries in which overhead projectors and computer runs presented general policies that did not leave much room for discretionary behavior and special exceptions. It was equally difficult for the political parties, which had neglected to adapt their ideology and rhetoric to changing international and local realities, to develop a coherent ideological alternative to the economic policies they did not support. Their ideological approach did not appear useful as a source for practical answers to the country's problems.

All of this is not meant to imply that the opposition was completely neutralized or incapable of effective action. In fact, the experience lends further support to the notion that in processes of change it is almost impossible to predict the sources, directions, and strengths of the forces resisting or distorting change. It is indeed a mazelike process full of surprises in which apparently very threatening actors turn out to be paper tigers, while unexpected minotaurs impose reversals and costly detours. Trade reform, the lifting of controls on interest rates, and the price increases on medicines and gasoline are examples of such cases.

Strong doubts persisted within and outside of the government as to its capacity to impose and maintain the trade liberalization program. Stiff resistance was offered by the private sector, unions, and the political parties. Nevertheless, not only was trade reform implemented as planned, but it also was extended to incorporate the agricultural sector in a much earlier stage and with more profound reforms than originally envisaged. On the other hand, while it certainly was known that the substantial increase in interest rates was going to be painful, no one had anticipated that the reaction would oblige the government to reverse and revise its decisions in this domain. In practice, the Supreme Court of Justice obliged the Central Bank to reverse its decision to free interest rates (see endnote 15) and intense public protests backed by a strong political coalition and Congress imposed a new and sizable subsidy for interest payments on all home mortgages. Another interesting example was that the strong protests over the increases in medicine prices did not lead to a restitution of price control in medicines, yet the political turmoil and opposition to the hikes in the price of gasoline effectively impeded and stalled further increases for more than two years.

But the Venezuelan experience also shows that changes tend to be delayed and distorted not only as a consequence of the need to receive Congressional approval or to transform the organizations in the process of their implementation. It also shows that even when the reforms fall within the purview of the Executive Branch, speed and precision in their execution tended to depend on the political origin of the minister in charge of administering the changes. This experience shows that in those areas in which the responsible official had strong political affiliations with the ruling party, change tended to be either slower, somewhat different from what had been agreed to or planned, or, in some instances, merely cosmetic. In fact, an interesting point to note was that other than Congress, the strongest and most effective source of opposition to the reforms was found within the cabinet—among ministers appointed on the basis of party affiliation or loyalty. In the Venezuelan case, the reforms could proceed without major distortions or delays because these change-resisting ministers were in a minority and President Pérez was strongly committed to the reforms.

Given that the dynamics of assembling a cabinet often require a dose of compromise and negotiation, the ministers seldom form a coherent body with a common view about priorities and restrictions. Therefore, if there is not a strong, clearly dominant coalition of ministers with a common perspective as well as an equally strong presidential leadership, the situation is destined to deteriorate into one in which each subgroup of ministers has enough power to block the initiatives of the other, but no single group is capable of imposing its own view. Obviously, under such circumstances the normal difficulties of coordinating the efforts aimed at producing large-scale societal change are greatly increased.

The Big Gap: The Institutional Nightmare of Social Policy Implementation

As noted above, the early stages of the Venezuelan experience show a striking and worrying trend of poverty-alleviation efforts lagging significantly behind in producing results, as compared to the successes in restoring macroeconomic equilibrium and, even more importantly, in relation to the objective needs and subjective expectations of the population. In fact, all available indicators show that inflation (especially in food prices), and the institutional collapse of traditional social services in education, health, nutrition, housing, and personal security did have a strong negative impact on the poor and that the government's efforts could not sufficiently counter such a result. Several factors account for this critical lag:

1. It can be convincingly argued that further deterioration in social conditions in Venezuela during 1990–1992 was a certainty given the existing trends of the economy. Paramount among these was the deeply ingrained inflationary pressure, the very nature of which made it impossible to neutralize altogether. In fact, it also seems warranted to assume that the reforms spared the country several years of even higher inflation and its impoverishing effects.

2. The nature of the new social policy orientation—with its reliance on the creation of stable, productive jobs, directly targeted subsidies, the building of a web of government and nongovernment organizations (NGOs) capable of providing an effective social safety net, and the general strengthening of the state's institutional capacity to design and implement sound social policies—requires a much longer time horizon for its evaluation than the one we are using in this chapter. More time is clearly needed to appraise the impact of the government's efforts at poverty alleviation and the net effect on social conditions of the new policy orientation.

3. With the two previous points as caveats, it bears noting that, although both in Venezuela and abroad much thought and research had gone into the design of the macroeconomic policy package, this was not the case for social policy. Furthermore, the center of the government's attention during the initial years of the reform program had a significant bias toward economic policy decisions aimed at avoiding the further macroeconomic deterioration and at the consolidation of the new policy framework. Although there were constant concerns about the social situation, and although significant efforts were directed at creating new social service, institutions (like the Beca Alimentaria and the maternal and infant nutrition programs), the reform efforts in the purely economic front absorbed most of the government's energies and attention.

In this sense, the Venezuelan experience does not seem unique. Social policies were not part of the policy package described as the "Washington Consensus,"[35] the model that inspired the design of the reforms in Venezuela and elsewhere in the developing world. The "consensus" was a prescription for macroeconomic stabilization and renewed growth that assumed that, without noninflationary growth and the systematic creation of stable employment, efforts directed toward the poor would generally be wasted. Furthermore, in the words of one of the better-known proponents of the approach:

> The policies subsumed under the "Washington consensus" are not by themselves likely to lead to a substantial or rapid improvement in income distribution. If we worry about equity, we need to be able to count on more than trickle down benefits. We need a separate set of policy reforms addressed specifically to that issue.[36]

Although the intellectual and institutional apparatus that developed the macroeconomic stabilization policies and the structural reforms was very successful in promoting their adoption, there was not an equivalent effort at conceptualizing and promoting the adoption of practical policy prescriptions aimed at alleviating the social costs imposed by many years of misguided policies and by the corrections needed to restore economic normalcy. In fact, a World Bank document that reviewed the design and implementation of a sample of the Bank's "adjustment loans" in the 1980s concluded that:

> In many of the programs reviewed, alleviation of social costs, which has become increasingly important since the mid-1980's, seems to have been handled mainly as an afterthought rather than as an integral part of adjustment planning.[37]

The Venezuelan case was not included in the sample reviewed by that evaluation. But having learned from experience, a substantial amount of funds for the social sectors was made available in aid to the government from World Bank to support the country's reform efforts. Nevertheless, the weak institutional capacity of the state in that sector greatly inhibited rapid utilization of these funds. As we will see next, the complex nature of the policies greatly contributed to the implementation difficulties that the government faced in this respect.

4. The policies aimed at alleviating the social costs of the reform process were not only very novel in their approach, but also extremely complex in their implementation. In fact, they critically depended for their success on what the Venezuelan state lacked most: management. Targeting state aid to the poor means, in practice, the use of a massive direct marketing and distribution network capable of identifying and monitoring specific individuals and families, and systematically channeling goods and complex services such as health care to each one of them. The management literature is full of examples indicating that there are few tasks more challenging to modern corporations than establishing and operating a distribution system.[38] It is easy to imagine how much more daunting the task is for a government bureaucracy to distribute

basic staples to the most marginalized segments of society, instead of channeling products to consumers, to rely on the judgments made by underpaid and undertrained bureaucrats based on information that is seldom completely reliable, instead of using prices as mediating mechanisms.

This is not to say that the task is impossible, that its main emphasis is misplaced, or that past practices of indiscriminate and socially regressive generalized subsidies have something to offer at this juncture. The point is to stress the critical importance of incorporating social policy considerations into the design of the reform package from the beginning and devising mechanisms to insure that at least the same level of managerial talent and ministerial attention is given to this aspect of the reform process.

5. The Venezuelan experience also demonstrates that the need to generate the quick institutional response required to cushion the rapid social impact of macroeconomic corrections led to a generalized propensity to bypass existing and highly inefficient ministries and social services agencies through the use of ad hoc organizational arrangements and new institutions. While this strategy might have been the only viable alternative during the initial critical stages of the reform process, it is certainly not an adequate long-term solution to the paralysis to which many decades of mismanagement and political neglect have condemned traditional social service delivery agencies.

The proliferation of new institutions was also fueled by the trend toward decentralization and concomitant efforts of the newly elected state governors to gain control of social delivery agencies in their regions. These simultaneous trends created a disjointed, overlapping, and highly inefficient set of institutions over whose activities it became almost impossible for the weak existing ministries to exert any semblance of coordination and rationality. More than eighty different poorly coordinated public organizations are charged with health delivery and a roughly similar number intervene in education.[39]

This orientation, which made the rapid and direct transfer of resources to the poor the almost exclusive concern of the government's efforts, had the effect of distracting attention from the need to rapidly upgrade the capacity of the basic social service agencies. It also created the illusion that the social emergency the country was experiencing was being taken care of by the new social programs. An overwhelmed government, its managerial capacity stretched well beyond its limits and plagued by all sorts of institutional and political problems, found in the new social initiatives the escape valve through which it could relieve the pressures arising from the lack of practical answers to paralyzed hospitals, an educational system in shambles, an overcongested and inefficient public transportation system, and crime rates that had become an obsessive nightmare for all segments of society.

Accelerating the desperately needed progress in government performance with social programs will essentially depend on its success in restructuring and modernizing the "social" ministries (health, housing, labor, education, and so forth) and public services like police protection. In turn, the success of such restructuring will be critically determined by the state's capacity to curb the predatory relationship that political parties, unions, professional associations, and other vested interests have developed with the social service delivery institutions. Such capacity is usually found in stronger and more autonomous states than what has hitherto been the case in Venezuela.

The Private Sector: Expecting Too Much, Too Soon

Never before in its history had the Venezuelan government placed so much faith and transferred so much responsibility to the private sector as it did in the 1989 reforms. Price liberalization, privatization, trade reform, the opening of foreign direct investment, the sweeping deregulation of entire economic sectors, and even the reliance on private NGOs for the provision of social services, have all made markets, entrepreneurship, and private investment critical factors for the success of the government's development strategy.

The early years of the Venezuelan experience show that in fact the private sector does appear willing and able to play a much larger role than the one to which it had been confined. That experience also demonstrates that great caution should be exerted when estimating the speed, nature, magnitude, and effects of the private sector's response. It also forcefully points to the need for the intelligent intertwining of state and market, and for a division of labor between the two that is better suited to deal with the new domestic and international realities.

The main risk is to burden the private sector with so many hopes, expectations, and responsibilities that frustration and disappointment are bound to ensue, thus setting the stage for a backlash that could truncate its potential to play a larger positive role. In particular, the Venezuelan case indicates that two central assumptions, commonly made in reference to the private sector's response to the new incentives generated by market-oriented reforms, should be carefully qualified. These assumptions are: (1) that the capital nationals have abroad constitutes a sound base on which the private sector can rapidly build the new, enlarged role envisioned in the new policy orientation; and (2) that the competitiveness of the local private sector, and its propensity to invest, are essentially a function of having an appropriate macroeconomic policy framework in place and an institutional environment enabling businessmen to conduct their affairs efficiently and profitably. Let us briefly examine these two assumptions.

Some Venezuelans do own large amounts of capital deposited abroad, and it seems safe to assume that a portion of that capital is available for investments in the country. In fact, in the first years of the reform program more capital entered the country than was exported. But it also seems valid to assume that the ownership structure of that capital generates impediments and frictions to its mobility, in turn constraining the size of the foreign assets owned and available in the medium term for investment in Venezuela.

Specifically, we have to assume that there is a portion of foreign assets owned by former public officials, politicians, union leaders, and others who cannot legally justify such ownership. Therefore, for these "underground capitalists" investing in the country implies the added risk of exposing to the public their ties to assets they cannot justify controlling. This means their capital will face higher than normal risks if reinvested in the country, implying that only projects with rates of return capable of compensating these additional risks will be attractive to them. Projects like these are not that common, and even if found, the investment vehicle to be used will be required to provide complete anonymity for the investors without at the same time excessively eroding their ownership rights. These requirements, along with the reasonable assumption that, with regard to their foreign holdings, these individuals are rentiers more than businesspeople, also add to the impediments to repatriation of this capital: they do not possess the attitudes and entrepreneurial skills needed to identify business opportunities and adequately structure their participation.

The other segment of the population that can be safely assumed to hold significant amounts of flight capital is the business community. Here also it is possible to identify obstacles to capital repatriation. The principal obstacle stems from the fact that the new business conditions imposed by market-oriented reforms require different entrepreneurial talents and organizational skills than those used under the high-protection, high-subsidization, low-competition scheme that prevailed in the past. Although a new generation of more aggressive and competitive entrepreneurs is emerging and taking advantage of the new opportunities, a portion of the business community has simply lost its ability to turn a profit under new conditions of heightened domestic and international competition. Given the risk-return relationship of their foreign holdings and of their direct investments in the country, in the short and perhaps even medium term a bias against capital repatriation for direct investment purposes is not surprising. The chairman of an important business group in Venezuela expressed this bias bluntly and cogently:

> Since our beginning, in the early sixties, the government had always protected and offered us all sorts of special incentives. It's true that it

also controlled our prices and made life difficult in many other ways, but on balance it created conditions for us and others to grow and prosper. We never had to worry a whole lot about foreign competition and the exchange rate made it impossible for us to even attempt to export. Since we began, exports had never been a government priority and for thirty years it was obvious that creating employment and supplying the local markets was all that was expected from us. Now, all of a sudden, the new government tells us not only that interest rates will be three times higher, and that the price we pay for electricity will also increase threefold, but that the protection against cheaper foreign products will be taken away from us and that we will have to be able to compete internationally and start exporting. In order to do that I will have to do two things: One is to bring back several million dollars, buy new machinery and modernize our operation, making it more efficient, and the other is to buy myself and my people new suitcases and start travelling around the world trying to sell my products in competition with the Taiwanese and the Koreans, who, by the way, have been doing it for decades before us. On top of all this, of course, I will be risking the possibility that a new government, or even a new team in this same government, will change the policies and let the exchange rate appreci- ate and wipe out any competitive gains that we may have achieved.

At the same time, our holdings abroad not only are safe and without risks in comparison to our local operations, but each year they generate more profits than we can ever dream of making here, and this without having to worry about the government, the unions or the Taiwanese. (Conversation with the author; 1989)

Perhaps the most damaging collateral effect of capital flight has been this sterilization of the entrepreneurial impulses of a segment of the domestic private sector. On the other hand, given the high concentration of capital and economic activity in the private sector, the firms and individuals that have maintained a competitive spirit and are actively pursuing new opportunities also face organizational constraints in the short run on the number of operations that they can pursue. Although their access to the capital needed to fund new ventures may not be a problem for them, the lack of organizational support for the process imposes limits on the speed and orientation with which that capital can be utilized and new opportunities exploited.

All of these considerations confirm the extraordinary importance of reliable, efficient, and transparent domestic capital markets and, espe- cially, stock markets to ensure freer return of capital. These, together with a judicial system that can be relied upon to enforce contracts and protect property rights, constitute two fundamental elements of an enabling environment for private investment, without which capital repatriation will be slower and more expensive for society.

But efficient stock markets, a reliable judicial system, and a stable macroeconomic environment may not be sufficient to attract the interest of local private investors. Opportunities are also required, and under the new policy framework profitable opportunities tend to require a substantial degree of competitiveness. Firms have to be capable of successfully competing with imports, with foreign firms in the local market, or with world players in international markets. As noted, the past experience of Venezuelan corporations did not hone such competitiveness. At least in the foreseeable future, therefore, new business initiatives will have to rely heavily on the role of foreign companies that have the technology, marketing skills, and access to international markets needed to succeed in the new environment. This situation points to the well-established importance of direct foreign investment as a critical catalytic factor in the economic restructuring of reforming countries. But it also points to a major unresolved question for policymakers in those countries, namely, the role of the state in supporting the development of the private sector in the industries in which it is believed that the country has or can have an advantage over its international competitors.

One side in the debate on this question points that the success of countries like Japan and East Asia's newly industrialized countries (NICs), for example, in developing strong export sectors. According to this argument, their success was achieved by targeting specific sectors, channeling a plethora of subsidies and incentives to private firms in those sectors, and finally, ensuring the sustained direct attention of an active set of government agencies working in complex and close partnership with the private sector.[40] The opposing camp points to the many countries in which the government's selection of priority industrial sectors only served to make a small number of entrepreneurs and their friends in government very rich and the competitiveness of the selected sectors very poor.[41]

In its initial phase, the Venezuelan experience in this regard demonstrates that:

1. The government lacked the political strength and autonomy to develop an industrial policy based on an objective and independent selection of priority sectors. The government's capacity to eliminate tariff protections and other subsidies to the private sector was due in large measure to the fact that, for the most part, it was done transparently and affected every industrial sector more or less equally. The government soon realized that its only hope for successfully resisting the myriad pressures for exceptions and demands for special treatment on the grounds of "national priority" was to maintain a strong commitment to sectoral neutrality. The bottom line was that it became clear that the eventual selection of specific industries for government support would ultimately be more a function of political influence than of the real or potential competitiveness of the chosen sectors.

2. Even in the absence of political interference and assuming that

outside consultants could provide an objective and rigorous assessment of what sectors, under the new policies, had the potential to become internationally competitive, the government lacked the institutions required to implement an industrial strategy of the East Asian NIC variety. The level of technical skills on the part of government officials and of intra- and interinstitutional coordination and commitment such a strategy requires clearly transcends the present capacities of Venezuela and perhaps of most other Latin American countries.

3. Venezuelan firms that are actively pursuing export strategies are having great difficulty entering foreign markets, regardless of how competitive they are. Even in the case of one of the least protectionist countries in the industrialized world, the United States, Venezuelan exports have recently been blocked by fourteen different legal actions initiated by, or at the request of, US firms seeking to protect their markets. Although some of these actions have been overruled by GATT or by US courts, it is estimated that these actions alone have cost Venezuelan firms over $400 million per year in lost potential earnings.[42] Exporting to other markets is also proving to be greatly hampered by subtle and not-so-subtle protectionist practices common to many countries and by the competitive advantage that other firms have due to longer experience, greater resources, or the capacity of their governments to effectively support them in their international activities. Meanwhile, as the domestic economy recovers its import capacity and tariff protection continues its scheduled decline, complaints of local producers about the dumping practices of foreign exporters to Venezuela continue to mount.

4. International experience shows that a country's achievements in terms of competitiveness are usually preceded by effective efforts in professional education and vocational training.[43] In Venezuela, as in many other countries of the region, the results of such efforts are greatly constrained by the institutional devastation of the country's public universities and training centers. Such devastation is not due to lack of funds. Venezuela boasts the highest level of per capita expenditure for public education in Latin America, and 55 percent of this budget is spent on higher education, which represents 7.5 percent level of total student enrollment. Only 27 percent is spent on primary schools, which include 68 percent of all the students served by the educational system.[44] Universities also suffer from the same problems of congestion, clientelistic politics, isolation, and mismanagement plaguing other social institutions in the country. They also have been captured by powerful unions and other internal groups that have been very effective in resisting the changes threatening their long-established privileges. Under such circumstances, the possibility of developing a mutually supportive relationship between the country's efforts in higher education and training and those aimed at enhancing its international competitiveness hinge on the

government's capacity to minimize the interference of the small but powerful groups deriving significant benefits from the control they exert in higher educational institutions.

The central message of the four points listed above is that major unresolved questions exist as to how to reconcile the political, technical, and institutional limitations of providing Venezuelan private firms with the direct government support most of their international competitors enjoy. And this has to be done without reliving the sorry experience of the past, when targeting industries essentially had a soporific effect on their competitive drive.

As was the case for the hopes for a more effective social policy, any answer in this respect must take into account the need for building a stronger, better managed, more autonomous state.

Conclusions: Bringing Back Ideology and the State

Will the reforms last? If so, how much deeper into the market-oriented, export-based strategy will the country be taken? Or what can be done to ensure that an eventual process of reforming the reforms will not lead to repetition of the costly mistakes made in the past?

Answers to these questions tend to focus on the assessment of the "political will" to stay the course and on the power and popularity of the president. In theory, "political will" ensures that unpopular but necessary decisions will be made and presidential power seems necessary to effectively shield the economic team from "undue" political interference and to ensure a more technocratically correct execution of the reforms.

Although these answers can perhaps provide a useful assessment of the situation, they are obviously manifestations of other more profound determinants of the future stability of the reforms.

In fact, it can be argued that the main determinants of the maintenance of the reforms are, together with their performance, the degree to which their main tenets can be more firmly anchored in society and the degree to which a stronger state more capable of autonomous and efficient action can emerge.

In this sense, two important common misperceptions need to be corrected. The first is the impression that the adoption of market-oriented policy reforms in almost all countries of the region is based on a widely disseminated and deeply ingrained ideological transformation as part of a worldwide trend. The second is that the new policies essentially call for the dismantling of the state apparatus and its reduction to a minimal structure in charge of public functions as narrowly defined as possible.

As we saw, the main impulse behind the Venezuelan reform program was the urgent need to provide practical answers to immediate macroeconomic problems that could no longer be ignored. This impetus toward macroeconomic stabilization opened the possibility for broader reforms, which prompted other sweeping changes in the nation's political, economic, social, and institutional landscape.

It was also noted that the fact that the changes gave such an unprecedented role to the market is less a result of a newfound commitment to capitalism than the disrepute of previous state-centered schemes (and their Venezuelan proponents) that were perceived as responsible for the "lost decade"; the positive example of other countries in Asia and Latin America; the collapse of the USSR and the Eastern European bloc; and, last but not least, the seductive attraction of billions of dollars in desperately needed economic assistance offered by multilateral financial agencies and industrialized countries contingent upon the adoption of market-oriented reforms. This is not to say that traditional ideas, beliefs, and prejudices have not been revised and changed and that no ideological shift has taken place amongst certain circles. The point is that ideological change was not the main force driving the reforms.

The fact is that in Venezuela, as in almost all reforming countries in Latin America, the market-oriented policies are being pursued almost singlehandedly by a committed but politically isolated president, with the support of multilateral institutions, a cabinet formed mainly by outsiders, and the passive—and sometimes not so passive—resistance of the governing party. Society at large has not been mobilized in support of the reforms—much to the contrary, severe hardships and very low living standards have continued. While it can be argued that the reforms were the only option to reverse the downward spiral and that there can now be hope for some improvement, these are remote and not very convincing abstractions for the great majority of the population. Furthermore, in contrast to the recognition and praise that the Venezuelan reforms occasionally receive in the international media, local public opinion is constantly bombarded through the domestic media with negative images of the country's situation that, while undoubtedly reflecting reality, also reflect the complex interplay of media editors and owners with the government in pursuit of their own vested interests.[45]

Cementing the changes will require a far greater degree of social and political acceptance, which can be expected to increase gradually as larger groups of society begin to experience an improvement in their living conditions. But regardless of the policies' performance, their permanent grounding cannot succeed without a deeper and wider social acceptance of the legitimacy of their aims and of the instruments utilized to achieve them. An indispensable and in Venezuela hitherto ignored complement of the economic stabilization and restructuring efforts is the building of a broader, less technocratic, shared vision of the future. As Senge[46] has noted in another context, it is necessary to unearth shared "pictures of the future" to foster genuine commitment and enrollment rather than compliance. This is of course one of the roles of ideology. Ideology breeds patience and tolerance for the insufficiencies and short-comings of any given model of social organization and political action.

The broader social acceptance of the previous state-centered model explains Venezuelans' tolerance and patience with the many financial scandals that the country witnessed, the continuously deteriorating living standards, the massive yearly losses of inefficient state-owned enterprises, and the corrupt and inefficient state.

While it can be demonstrated that the previous policy orientation had all sorts of defects, and in fact could not be sustained, two major factors account for its longevity. The first is that while the system generated declining living conditions and poverty for the great majority, it concentrated enormous wealth among many politicians, union leaders, opinionmakers, and businessmen. The second is that the policies had a solid grounding in the ideological tenets of all the main political parties in the country. Most active politicians in the country—and also some private sector leaders and most journalists and academics—had come to share basic hopes and expectations about the role of the state and a fundamental mistrust of the market. These attitudes, of course, not only flowed out of ideological convictions, but in many cases became firmly cemented by the great personal gains that these individuals were deriving from the existing state of affairs.

Neither of these two elements—the ideological conviction or broad popular benefit—is yet present in the Venezuelan context. The reforms are, in fact, attempting to eliminate many of the policy-induced economic distortions that generated the myriad opportunities for these influential groups to make large fortunes through the political intermediation of economic and business decisions. The new policies' explicit aim is to broaden the base of the beneficiaries of the country's developmental efforts.

In terms of building ideological commitment, the current policy framework is too recent, too "narrow or technical," and too "foreign" to elicit the active support that the previous policy orientation enjoyed. It can be argued that too much is being asked from a scheme developed to deal with macroeconomic problems and structural distortions of the economy. In practice, the economic stabilization program was expected to provide effective answers to the many noneconomic questions that society was facing and thereby fill the political and ideological vacuum left by the perceived failure of the previous policies and the disrepute of those charged with implementing them.

The point is that the economic program has had to perform political functions for which it was not designed and for which it is ill-suited. The design of the economic program does not allow for the guidance, the goals, and the powerful recruitment, enrollment, and political mobilization functions that a broader, more politically and ideologically grounded program can supply.

In the absence of a broader social and political consensus, policy stability will continue to depend on: the ineffectiveness of opposing groups to provide credible alternative strategies, the legitimization of market-oriented reforms through the demonstration effect of other countries, the unwavering personal commitment of the president and his close collaborators, the support of foreign investors and the more competitive segments of the local private sector, the support of multilateral institutions, and the effectiveness and speed of the policies in achieving their stated goals.

The stability of the reforms will be continuously tested by events that might have been tolerated in the past. However, under the current circumstances of "adjustment fatigue," an ideological vacuum, and political support by default, such events will pose much greater challenges and risks. In an ideological vacuum patience is bound to be an increasingly scarce commodity.

The new market-centered policy scheme is also likely to have its share of scandals as the financial sector is deregulated at a pace exceeding the state's capacity to build its supervisory functions. The country is also likely to witness major regulatory failures as public utilities are privatized and the performance of the newly created regulatory agencies lags behind, as a feeble public sector attempts to deal for the first time ever with problems of extraordinary technical, economic, and legal complexity. The "illusion of harmony" will definitively be broken as the frequency and stridency of strikes and social unrest could reach levels unprecedented in the recent experience of the country, sparked by government efforts to restructure nonperforming public agencies employing large numbers of workers with very active unions. The new policy framework will also have to accommodate mounting complaints about the slowness with which benefits begin to trickle down and income and wealth begin to be more evenly distributed. Reformers will also have to withstand the political consequences of mistakes and policy errors that are almost certain for any government that tries to implement so many profound and complex changes at the same time, without a strong organizational, informational, and institutional base on which to execute the changes. These are shortcomings that seem more or less unavoidable and that are going to play a major part in shaping collective attitudes vis-à-vis the reforms and their stability.

A deeper ideological grounding of the reforms, however, will not be sufficient to ensure more policy stability in the absence of a stronger,

85

more efficient state. Emphasizing the market does not mean dismantling the state. In fact, as we discussed, a strong private sector cannot exist without a state capable of efficiently and intelligently executing an immense array of very complex tasks. The state should be capable of designing and implementing a consistent set of macroeconomic and sectoral policies, and it must have the capacity to create and sustain an economic and institutional environment that, while enabling private businesses to efficiently pursue profit opportunities, is also capable of ensuring the proper operation of markets and adequate regulation of private economic activity.

As we saw, for the reforms to be successful—and stable—major progress should be achieved in the implementation of social policies, which also requires the existence of a stronger state more capable of independent action. The supply and supervision of the infrastructure, which cannot be provided by the private sector in the quantity or the opportunity required by the country's needs, is another major task that the state will have to perform with great efficiency.

These are ideal, ambitious goals for any state. In practice, few modern states can claim a great deal of success in all of these functions. Perhaps states that have recently reformed their economies and are in the process of redesigning their public sector and rebuilding their institutional framework have a good opportunity to learn from their past mistakes and those of other countries in this arena of change. In the Venezuelan case, three deeply rooted state characteristics forcefully emerge as important obstacles for the reconstruction of a state with better developmental possibilities:

1. The public bureaucracy is being utilized as a functional substitute for the nonexistent safety net for the unemployed. Over the years, the politicization of this process and the growing incapacity of the economy to create stable and productive jobs has gradually eroded the notion that the main function of a public organization is to perform a specific task and not to provide politically mandated jobs. Unless this trend begins to be gradually reversed, discharging the complex functions that a modern state calls for will be greatly impaired.

2. The political role assigned to public employment, the lack of trained personnel in the country, and the poor working conditions in the public sector impose severe limits on the capacity of the Venezuelan state to attract, retain, and develop talented workers. Fiscal constraints, the antistate mood, and the generalized assumption that pay increases in the public sector would essentially benefit undeserving political appointees, have all made it very difficult to improve working conditions and attract the talent and leadership that the country desperately needs. For example, public salaries declined by 40 percent in real terms from

1985 to 1989. The maximum monthly salary for a professional working for the government was US $415 in 1990, while the basic monthly salary for a minister in 1991 was about US $900.[47]

Generating organizational structures and management practices, notably personnel policies for the public sector that are consistent with the new policy orientation, will certainly be an important source of policy stability.

3. The third trait exhibited by the Venezuelan state that needs even more profound changes than have yet been effected in these initial stages of the reform process relates to its capacity for autonomous action. Historically the public sector, rich with oil resources and without a well-developed political system, has been easy prey for groups pursuing particular narrow interests. Public income from oil has traditionally been sufficient to accommodate the demands and expectations of the wide array of special interest groups with the capacity to extract a share of oil rents from the state. This has created a predatory structure of groups linked to the state that over time has greatly constrained its capacity for the autonomous formulation and implementation of policies. One of the substantial contributions of the reforms initiated in 1989 was to demonstrate that under certain circumstances it was not impossible for the Venezuelan state to identify and implement policies aimed at improving the well-being of society as a whole, and that it was indeed possible to exclude and ignore the interests of the special groups that for years had monopolized the benefits of the government's efforts.

The challenge for the future is to build a political system and state in which the capacity to ignore the interest of small but influential groups will no longer be a rare phenomenon concentrated in a few areas of government action. Rather, it would be a normal characteristic of a state capable of defending the interest of the unorganized majority against the voraciousness of highly organized and influential minorities.

Notes

The author was the Venezuelan minister of Industry during the initial two years of the reform process discussed in this chapter, and was recently an executive director at the World Bank in Washington, D.C. All the information and data contained in the following pages is derived from published sources and public documents. The findings, interpretations, and conclusions expressed in this chapter are entirely those of the author and should not be attributed in any manner to the government of Venezuela or the World Bank. The author wishes to thank Joseph S. Tulchin, Armeane Choksi, Jonathan Coles, Rudiger Dornbusch, Judith Evans, Ricardo Hausmann, Robert R. Kaufman, Robert Klitgaard, Emilio Pacheco, Miguel Rodríguez, Jeffrey Sachs, Francisco Sagasti, and Strobe Talbott for their detailed and useful comments on previous versions of this chapter.

1. For an interesting review of Venezuela's macroeconomic evolution in the twentieth century, see Gustavo Escobar, "El Laberinto de la Economía," in Moisés Naím and Ramón Piñango, eds. *El Caso Venezuela: Una Ilusión de Armonía,* (Caracas: Ediciones IESA, 1974); Ricardo Hausmann, *Shocks Externos y Ajuste Macroeconómico,* (Caracas: Central Bank of Venezuela, 1990); and Antonio Francés, *Venezuela Posible,* (Caracas: Ediciones IESA, 1990). Unless otherwise indicated, the sources for the statistics used in this paper are the Central Bank of Venezuela Annual Report and the Central Office for Statistics and Informatics (OCEI), various years, *Encuesta Industrial,* (Caracas: OCEI); several World Bank reports: *Venezuela: A Review of the 1990–1993 Public Sector Investment Program,* Report no. 8588-VE (Washington: World Bank, 1990); *Venezuela Poverty Study: From Generalized Subsidies to Targeted Programs,* Report no. 9114-VE (Washington: World Bank, 1991); *Venezuela: Public Administration Study,* Report no. 8972 (Washington: World Bank, 1991); *The Challenge of Development: World Development Report 1991* (Oxford: Oxford University Press, 1991); and International Monetary Fund (IMF), various years, *International Financial Statistics,* (Washington: IMF).

2. See Alan Gelb and François Bourguignon, "Venezuela: Absorption Without Growth," in Alan Gelb, ed., *Oil Windfalls: Blessing or Curse?* (Oxford: Oxford University Press, 1988); and Ricardo Hausmann, "Dealing with Negative Oil Shocks: The Venezuelan Experience in the Eighties." Paper presented at the Conference on Temporary Trade Shocks held at St. Anthony's College, Oxford, 1991.

3. Between 1975 and 1979 productivity decreased an average of 1.1 percent each year and from 1983 to 1988 the decline accelerated to 1.4 percent per year. The productivity of industrial sectors in which state-owned enterprises were dominant decreased 9.2 percent per year during the late seventies and 1.4 percent per year from 1983 to 1988. From 1979 to 1983, productivity grew at 5.2 percent per year, thus making its average 0.7 percent for the period from 1975 to 1988. During this time, the productivity of South Korea was growing at 9 percent per year, that of Argentina at almost 3 percent, and that of Mexico at about 2 percent. See World Bank *Venezuela: Industrial Sector Report,* Report no. 9028-VE (Washington: World Bank, 1991).

4. For an elaboration of this point and its consequences in shaping many aspects of contemporary Venezuelan society, see Moisés Naím and Ramón Piñango, eds., *El Caso Venezuela: Una Ilusión de Armonía* (Caracas: Ediciones IESA, 1974), p. 538ff.

5. See Ricardo Hausmann, *Shocks Externos y Ajuste Macroeconómico* (Caracas: Central Bank of Venezuela, 1990), p. 333ff.

6. The World Bank, *Venezuela Poverty Study: From Generalized Subsidies to Targeted Programs,* Report no. 9114-VE. (Washington: World Bank, 1991); and William R. Cline and Jonathan Conninge, *Venezuela: Economic Strategy and Prospects* (Washington: Inter-American Development Bank, 1992).

7. Many explanations have been advanced about this tragic episode and its determinants. Although this is not the place to attempt a detailed analysis of these events, it is useful to offer at least a few facts about them that will also serve to illustrate the conditions under which major policy changes had to be implemented:

- The riots erupted spontaneously. There was no organization that deliberately induced people to protest. The triggering factor was that the 27th, the last Monday of the month, workers living in the outskirts of Caracas went, like any other day, to take the small buses that transported them to the city and to their jobs. That day however, they were surprised by a substantial increase in the fare, part of which was authorized by the government and part of which was unilaterally decided by the individual owners-drivers of the buses. They felt that the new fares authorized by the government were largely insufficient to cover all the cost increases that they had been experiencing in the several previous months. This generated heated arguments between the drivers and their passengers that soon escalated to angry protests and then to widespread scuffles. The situation was clearly exacerbated by the fact that being the end of the month, workers were low on cash, and many had just the bare minimum to cover the usual fares so that they could collect their paychecks.

- Once the scuffles and violence started it became very obvious that the police were not capable of intervening effectively. They lacked the manpower, equipment, training, and organizational capacity to react to the situation. What was not widely known at the time was that the Caracas Metropolitan police department was in the midst of its most severe institutional crisis ever, having just ended the first strike in its history the week before. Many years of budget cuts had left the force with insufficient resources, deep morale problems, and without the institutional capacity to provide a city of 5 million inhabitants with the police services it needed. At the time of the riots, the issues that had prompted the strike were still unresolved. Furthermore, the DISIP, a national police force originally created to serve the intelligence needs of the government, was also undergoing a major institutional crisis and was in the midst of a complete overhaul that essentially rendered it ineffective for several months.

- The scuffles, fights, and protests over the fare increases led to looting episodes in which small groups of protesters would smash store windows and pillage whatever they could find. These started as isolated events, but as the day proceeded without any major police intervention and with growing numbers of people participating in these events, the situation rapidly escalated to the looting of many supermarkets and even factories located near the poor neighborhoods surrounding Caracas.

- The impunity with which all these events were taking place was being broadcast live on radio and television, thus prompting those not originally involved in the looting episodes to take to the streets. During the first day and before the government ordered the army to intervene, people could see on their television sets that it was just a matter of going to their nearby shopping center, entering the abandoned and opened stores, and taking whatever was left.

- The president postponed for as long as he could the decision to call in the army and decree a curfew and the temporary suspension of constitutional guarantees that eventually lasted ten days. He was aware that the army was not trained to deal with episodes of civil disobedience and that its involvement was bound to be traumatic. At the same time, he entered into a systematic series of urgent consultations with all parties represented in Congress, with labor and private sector leaders, as well as with a wide variety of other representative groups to seek their support for the actions needed to regain control of the situation. This effort was both necessary and successful, but it took almost a day and a half, a period during which no effective government presence was felt in the streets. This contributed to a deepening of the perceptions of impunity with which rioters were acting, and to the demonstration effect that also fueled the events.

89

- As will be discussed below, during the last part of 1988 and early 1989 the population had been subjected to the most severe shortages of consumer goods it had ever experienced. This created major tensions between consumers and merchants who either did not have the merchandise or were not willing to sell it, waiting for the government to authorize higher prices.

8. Although the list of items under price control changed over time, the more the government felt that inflation was getting out of control, the longer the list became. This did not mean, however, that the system was immune to periodic price hikes on the controlled products. These sudden and sometimes very large price increases became essentially dependent on the producers' bargaining power, which not surprisingly was itself a function of their political contacts and their willingness and capacity to bribe Ministry of Development and other officials. The last version of the price control regime had been established in 1987 and was one of the most restrictively administered the country ever had. There were forty-three broad categories (for example, medicines) for which producers could not alter prices without the official approval of the Ministry. For the rest, every price increase had to be reported to the Ministry, which then had the authority, to deny it. Items under severe price controls were not only goods like bread, milk, medicines, and such. They also included, for example, a cup of coffee at any coffee shop (with two different prices, depending on whether it was drunk standing at a counter or sitting at a table), all restaurant menus, tickets to movie theaters, ice, funeral services (two different options), toothpaste, batteries, spaghetti, foam for matteresses, soft drinks, toilet paper (three varieties), auto parts, beer, and so forth. See *Gaceta Oficial,* "Decreto 1977," (Caracas: Imprenta Nacional, 1986) p. 143.

9. For most of 1988, all key decisionmakers within the government were repeatedly notified by their superiors that everyone had to adopt what was half-jokingly referred to as "the X-ray exam" posture: don't move; hold your breath; and wait for the election.

10. As was indicated in note 4 above, the social tensions that had accumulated during the last months of 1988, and that were closely associated with the shortages of basic consumer goods, greatly contributed to the social atmosphere in which the February 1989 riots were bred.

11. The fiscal deficit was also determined by the fact that the legal framework that ruled the process of public budget construction generated an institutional setting that made attempts at rationalizing government spending almost futile. Furthermore, the fact that the Ministry of Public Finance (Hacienda) had, for more than a decade, as its main organizational objectives the negotiation of the foreign debt and the "administration" of the foreign exchange regime, greatly weakened its capacity to manage efficiently the country's public finances. This function over the years suffered continuous decay in its administration as oil revenues provided the funds to compensate for administrative inefficiencies.

12. For ten years after his first presidency, Pérez conducted intense international political activity that, by putting him in contact with a wide group of world leaders, allowed him to witness closely the changes in ideas and actions that were occurring almost everywhere, thus setting the stage for his own actions. Furthermore, while no specific individual can be singled out as having had a major influence in Pérez's new thinking, the intimate exposure he had to the government experiences of two of his closest personal and political friends undoubtedly played a major role in shaping his new vision. The lessons derived from the catastrophic failures of Alan García in Peru and the successful reforms of Felipe

González in Spain were not lost on Carlos Andrés Pérez.

13. It is worth noting that the appointment to cabinet posts of independent "technocrats," recruited from think tanks, universities and, in general, from professionally oriented organizations as opposed to the ruling party, has become a standard feature in most Latin American and Eastern European countries that have introduced major policy reforms.

14. See John Williamson, "What Washington Means by Policy Reform," in John Williamson, ed., *Latin American Adjustment: How Much Has Happened?* (Washington: Institute for International Economics, 1990).

15. The Central Bank was sued by an individual who claimed that the Bank's law obliged the Bank to fix the upper and lower limits for interest rates and that, therefore, the Bank's decision to let the market determine the rates was illegal. The Supreme Court agreed and the Bank had to reverse its decision. The Central Bank then defined a sufficiently wide margin between the two limits to allow supply and demand to determine interest rates. The financial sector reform includes a new Central Bank law that eliminates the requirement for the Bank to fix interest rates.

16. For an analysis of Venezuela's debt renegotiation utilizing a game-theoretic approach, see Eva Guerón, "Las Estructuras de Negociación en la Renogociación de la Deuda Externa de Venezuela," (Caracas: Instituto de Estudios Politícos, Mimeo, 1992).

17. Pedro Augustín Palma, "Una Nueva Politíca Económica en Venezuela." Paper presented at the seminar "Venezuela: Development Options for the 1990s." (Stockholm: Stockholm University, Latinamerika Institutet, 1990).

18. Ricardo Hausmann offers a comprehensive review and analysis of the macroeconomic dynamics of this adjustment process in: "The Big-Bang Approach to Macro Balance in Venezuela." Paper presented at the World Bank's EDI Senior Policy Seminar, "Latin America: Facing the Challenge of Adjustment and Growth," Caracas, IESA, 1990; and "Adoption, Management and Abandonment of Multiple Exchange Rate Regimes with Import Controls: The Case of Venezuela," paper presented at the Tenth Latin American Meeting of the Econometrid Society, Punto del Este, Uruguay, 1991.

19. The riots were not only traumatic because of their uncontrolled violence, the deaths, the injuries, and the economic losses that occurred. The fact that most grocery stores and supermarkets were pillaged and had to be closed made it very difficult for everyone, but especially for the poor, to gain access to basic staples for months afterward. Many of the small stores located in the poor sections of the cities where the riots occurred had great difficulty reopening and many never did.

20. The abnormal increase in nonoil exports in 1989 and 1990 was also propelled by three nonrecurrent factors: (1) a strong domestic recession, together with the high levels of inventory that firms had accumulated in anticipation of a devaluation and the fact that increases in the interest rate made it extremely costly to carry such inventories exerted strong pressures toward exports; (2) a substantial fiscal incentive to exporters was in place that together with the deep devaluation generated very high profit margins in exports; and (3) the existing system encouraged the overinvoicing of exports, thus amplifying and distorting the relevant statistical data. After 1989 the domestic economy entered into a strong growth phase and excessive inventories and output that had been exported were oriented toward the domestic market. Furthermore, the framework to stimulate exports was totally modified, thus eliminating marginal exporters and also the incentives to overinvoice that firms had in order to gain access to the fiscal incentives. All of this provides a more sound and less artificial setting

for any growth that the export sector may experience in the future.

21. The expansion of the oil, gas, and petrochemical sectors in which foreign firms are major investors is expected to generate about $5 billion in new investments. Expansion of the aluminum and other metal processing operations is expected to provide about $1.5 billion. New tourism ventures are estimated at about $1 billion, and the privatization of state-owned enterprises and utilities should mobilize about $4 billion. Furthermore, the liberalization and deregulation of the agricultural and financial services sectors is already attracting new inflows of foreign direct investment. The deregulation of the stock market also has resulted in renewed interest of international portfolio investors.

22. International Finance Corporation. *Emerging Stock Markets Factbook.* (Washington: International Finance Corporation, 1991).

23. In the future, a less comfortable situation regarding the current account of the balance of payments could emerge as a consequence of the trend toward higher imports determined by higher rates of economic growth and the potential for a decline in oil prices. The government hopes that the maintenance of a flexible, market-influenced exchange rate regime coupled with a sustained growth in exports as new outward-oriented investment projects mature, and the continuing inflow of foreign investment, will combine to ensure that the repetition of external sector crises like those of 1986 and 1989 are unlikely to occur.

24. See Hausmann, "Dealing with Negative Oil Shocks"; Cline and Conninge, *Venezuela;* and VENECONOMY, *Informe Mensual,* Caracas, June 1991.

25. Even in the early phases of the new foreign exchange regime, when the turbulence associated with extreme price instability, uncertainty, and all the structural changes were a major cause of concern, the exchange rate remained surprisingly stable. In 1990 and 1992, sudden changes in the exchange rate tended to be even more infrequent. In both of these years the maximum devaluation in a month was about 5 percent and, on average, the total yearly devaluation in the first three years was 20 percent.

26. An independent study of the exchange rate level based on the purchasing power parity (PPP) of the bolivar found that by mid-1991 the exchange rate was *undervalued* by about 6 percent, METROECONÓMICA, "Realidad del Sector Exportador no Tradicional," *Hechos y Tendencias de la Economía Venezolana,* Caracas, June 1991, p. 22. Another independent analysis using a different methodology concluded that the bolivar was *overvalued* by about 15 percent vis-à-vis the currencies of Venezuela's main trading partners (RK Asociados, *Síntesis Financiera,* June 1991).

27. Even the oil company, Petróleos de Venezuela (PDVSA), a paradigm of efficiency and professionalism among state-owned and even private multinational enterprises of the world, fell prey to the heightened expectations brought about by the increase in prices generated by the Gulf War. The company designed a five-year, $48 billion investment program aimed at maintaining its production potential and expanding its operations. Although the program was originally approved by the executive branch, it soon became evident that the macroeconomic implications of implementing such a program had not been sufficiently taken into account and that major revisions would have to be made. By mid-1991 and with the investment program just in its early, preparatory stages, PDVSA was pumping each day into the economy as much money as the rest of the public sector. This created a complex coordination problem given the Central Bank's restrictive monetary policy.

28. From mid-1989 to mid-1991, consumer prices increased 82 percent while the wholesale price index rose 47 percent (Cline and Conninge; 1992:24).

29. Marcelo Selowsky, "Etapas para la Reanudación del Crecimiento en

América Latina," *Finanzas y Desarrollo,* vol. 27, no. 2, June 1990.

30. World Bank, *Venezuela Poverty Study.*

31. World Bank, *The Challenge of Development: World Development Report 1991* (New York: Oxford University Press, 1991), pp. A4-A13.

32. Lance Taylor, *The Rocky Road to Reform,* forthcoming.

33. At the cabinet meeting in which the lifting of the exchange controls was discussed and eventually decided, two otherwise influential ministers argued vehemently, but ineffectively, in favor of retaining the controls. Their ineffectiveness in influencing that decision owed as much to their inability to articulate a solid economic argument as to the fact that during the preceding months much evidence had become available of the extreme corruption that had surrounded the functioning of the exchange control regime. It seems safe to assume that, had their views prevailed at the meeting, the adjustment would have taken much longer.

34. Research on the process through which large corporations adopt radical strategic changes also shows that it proceeds in stages that bear a striking resemblance to the process Venezuela went through in the 1980s. After a "denial period" in which justifications for avoiding changes are actively sought and minor adjustments are implemented without much success, a very confusing and conflict-ridden phase emerges in which the previous strategy is rejected and no other is formally adopted. This phase lasts until a loose coalition of individuals and groups identifies and articulates an alternative strategy, begins selling the new vision, and enlists the support of others. See Joseph Lorsch, "Managing Culture: The Invisible Barrier to Strategic Change," *California Management Review,* Winter 1986, p. 95; and Moisés Naím, "El Cambio en las Empresas Venezolanas," in Moisés Naím, ed., *Las Empresas Venezolanas: Su Gerencia* (Caracas: Ediciones IESA, 1989), p. 484.

35. Williamson, "What Washington Means."

36. Ibid., p. 4.

37. The World Bank, *Annual Review of Evaluation Results 1990,* Report no. 9870, (Washington: World Bank, 1991), pp. 3-21.

38. Alfred Chandler, *The Visible Hand* (Cambridge: Harvard University Press, 1977).

39. Moisés Naím and Ramón Piñango, eds., *El Caso Venezuela: Una Ilusión de Armonía* (Caracas: Ediciones IESA, 1974, p. 552; and Cline and Conninge, Venezuela, p. 103.

40. See, for example, Helen Shapiro and Lance Taylor, "The State and Industiral Strategy," *World Development,* vol. 18, no. 6, 1991; and Stephen C. Smith, *Industrial Policy in Developing Countries: Reconsidering the Real Sources of Export-Led Growth* (Washington: The Economic Policy Institute, 1991).

41. See Anne O. Krueger, "Government Failures in Development," *Journal of Economic Perspectives,* vol. 4, no. 3, Summer 1990; and World Bank, *The Challenge of Development.*

42. VENECONOMY, *Informe Semanal,* vol. 9, no. 43, Oct. 9, 1991; and *The Economist,* November 2, 1991.

43. See Colin Bradford and William Branson, eds., *Trade and Structural Change in Pacific Asia* (Chicago: University of Chicago Press, 1987); and Gary Gereffi, *Manufacturing Miracles* (New York: Duke University Press, 1990).

44. World Bank, *Venezuela Poverty Study,* p. x.

45. One of the often heard complaints in Venezuela as well as in most other reforming countries of the region concerns the weakness and ineffectiveness of the government's public communication efforts. Developing an intense media campaign to "educate" and "motivate" the population about the ways of the

market and about the need and justification for the new policies is frequently presented as one of the main priorities to which governments have not devoted sufficient attention.

46. Peter Senge, *The Fifth Discipline: The Art and Practice of the Learning Organization* (New York: Doubleday, 1990).

47. World Bank, *Venezuela Poverty Study,* 1991f, pp. 3, 35. In contrast, an academic earned about 1,200 dollars per month and a mid-career financial specialist from 1,300 to 1,900 dollars per month (World Bank, 1991c: 35). But low salaries are only a part of the problem. Possibilities for the normal development of professional careers are also very limited, and significant personal and professional risks exist for public officials because of very harsh laws designed to curb corruption but that in effect add all sorts of dangers for individuals holding decisionmaking posts. Furthermore, the rigid and primitive institutional framework for the management of human resources in the public sector that guides personnel practices also adds another dimension of complexity to the situation.

PART 3

THE INTERNATIONAL ARENA

5

The Reform of the State in Latin American Perspective

Carlos Blanco

For the past several years our continent has been in the throes of a complex and delicate crisis. For a particular contextual approach, we could focus on the onslaught of problems of external debt, which has now joined our countries in penury, the fluctuations in the prices of exportable raw materials, and the negligence of our governments. The question we must ask ourselves is why we were unable either to adequately anticipate what was approaching or to avail ourselves of the appropriate mechanisms with which to combat it. The underlying problem revolves around the fact that the economic crisis is related to the structural characteristics of Latin American societies, with a type of growth that has become inviable, and with a peculiar and progressively inadequate role in the world economy.

This particular style of consumption, production, investment, and distribution has proven inadequate. If the problems regarding exports and foreign debt were somehow reduced but no substantial internal changes in our economies were forthcoming, after a few years we would once again find ourselves face to face with the same ailments. Structural readjustment cannot be postponed. In other countries, war or their geopolitical posture at the international level served as the stimulus for their conversion. For us, that role is assumed by this crisis, which, even though its most brutal manifestations may abate, never really ceases to exist.

There is also a political crisis currently affecting the region, which is obscured for a variety of reasons by the economic situation. It sometimes settles the conscience of politicians to say that the crisis is merely economic in nature. The flourishing of democracy in Latin America leads many innocent souls to think we have emerged from the worst of our difficulties, but the process has not yet been concluded by any means. Both the old and the new democratic governments find themselves face to face with the problem of their viability, the problem of the governabil-

Carlos Blanco was the minister of State and the president of the Presidential Commission for State Reform of the Republic of Venezuela during the first years of the second Pérez administration.

97

ity of democracy. We can and must feel pride in the democratic progress achieved in the region, but it is nothing more than an excellent outlook, the product of both the aspirations of our peoples and the apparent futility of the "salvationist" authoritarianism that controls a large portion of the continent. Dictatorships in no way represent an escape from the crisis, and their so-called victories have been won on the basis of the ruination of their citizens.

Nevertheless, it has not yet been demonstrated that Latin American democracies are efficient enough to deal with the problems and challenges facing them. The situation is complex, since democratic progress has its place within the framework of a profound readjustment in the field of politics. The political parties, having historically undertaken the struggle for the conquest and consolidation of a regime based on individual freedoms, are experiencing a loss of representation. Many political parties are no longer the incarnation of the aspirations of struggle and mobilization of the masses, but rather representations of authoritarian forms of government. It never fails to produce a certain uneasiness to see how a few parties insist on clinging to ancient paradigms, even as they witness the collapse of the models that historically provided them with their inspiration.

This lack of far-reaching representativeness of many of the political parties is a critical element of the political panorama and a significant ingredient in the various derangements that the democratic system has been experiencing of late. Government institutions have also been affected by the growing loss of representativeness and are deteriorating. Many institutions, especially legislative and judicial bodies, the central administration, and public enterprises and institutions, have been undergoing a tremendous loss of credibility with the public. We often think that this loss of prestige is the result of a deliberate campaign by those who would reduce the state to an insignificant pile of ashes, but the truth is that such campaigns, when they indeed exist, are premised on undeniable realities. Institutionality has been profoundly weakened by its inefficiency, by its indifference to the private citizen, and by the erosion inflicted upon it by favoritism or "clientelism."

The convergence of the economic and political crises has led to the appearance of a social crisis totally without precedent in the region. We are not dealing merely with the long-standing phenomenon of impoverished masses. Democracy has always felt a sense of commitment to these social sectors and many of its policies have attempted to blunt the sharpest edges of poverty. We are now faced with a structural poverty that is growing and has the power to envelop the middle-class sectors of the population, which in many countries have been the product, and the most perfectly formed basis, of the democratic regime. We are dealing with a poverty no longer manifesting itself as a temporary insufficiency or breakdown, but rather as an expanding, structural ingredient of the reality of our societies. Worst of all, social policies conceived as superficial palliatives for the current circumstances not only fail to solve basic problems but occasionally tend to be factors in increasing the growth of the impoverished sectors of society.

In the midst of this situation there is ample room for decomposition, as expressed in a loss or absence of the values characteristic of a vigorous democracy. Corruption then becomes a practice that broadens its territory, eats away a major portion of the leadership, and leaves huge sectors of youth adrift. We are witness to a critical turning point in Latin America. If it is not dealt with properly, we run the risk of stagnation, or even a backslide of some consequence. The Latin American situation occurs within the framework of a worldwide process that is extremely suggestive and complex. Up until quite recently, a substantial portion of the Latin American intelligentsia sated itself on all the theoretical paradigms of the world. There were enough for all tastes and positions. But the conceptual mechanisms, labor union models, and classic examples are steadily being demolished. The conceptual arsenal with which many attempts were made to solve pressing problems has proven inefficient. Thus we are faced with the formidable dilemma of having to find the answers to today's challenges all by ourselves.

The relationship between politics and economics, between the state and civil society, between individual citizens and the community as a whole, has entered into a critical phase with regard to which the known mechanisms have demonstrated their weakness and untimeliness. The space for politics itself, so circumscribed and colonized by its quasi-private owners—the politicians—has been feeling the pressure to undergo substantial transformation. The reappropriation of politics by technicians, poets, and men and women of letters in many parts of the world is not a phenomenon that only exists anecdotally. Are we dealing with an "invasion" of politics or the disappearance of what until now has been a closed preserve, so as to give way to a reintegration of social spheres apparently split in two?

The East is being redefined. Together with the statues, a way of understanding power and society is also being torn down. Styles and models come to an end. But now is not the time to give that somewhat ingenuous cry of victory that is heard in certain regions of the West. Here also there will be changes, already foreshadowed in the formidable experiences of Europe, Asia, and North America. Perhaps the process being carried out in the two Germanies will give us a concise understanding of what is happening: the former German Democratic Republic is undergoing an astounding transformation, but the former Federal Republic of Germany is undergoing another, which is its counterpart in the same dimension.

Latin America, with its peculiar processes and rhythms, is affected by the same flow of worldwide change, has confronted similar inviable situations, and is besieged by the demands of its peoples as never before. Inexorably, Latin America will join this process. The discussion revolves around its ability to do so by its own means or as a result of the unleashing of blind tendencies that will colonize it once again. The continent forms part of the global wager in which the world itself is at stake—and we have no choice but to pick up the challenge.

The reforms the region is adopting are part of a crisis that is civilizing in nature. They are structural and cultural forms that have entered into a phase of revision and even collapse, forms of apprehension, a style of existence, ways in which to govern and participate. New forces are emerging and new codes and languages are coming into existence in such a way that the transformation we face implies not only processes and structures, but also the transformation of the very subjects of that change. The current worldwide atmosphere is favorable to those changes and to the need for Latin America to involve itself in these dynamics, as is dictated by its own crisis.

If we analyze our limitations and inabilities we quickly run up against the state, which in Latin America suffers from numerous characteristics hindering it from acting with sufficient flexibility to deal with today's challenges: centralism, partyism, clientelism, and the loss or lack of institutionality.

Centralism is not merely an administrative fact, but rather the way our societies historically tended to establish themselves as a product of the realities of national integration and the way resources tended to flow. This process, which acquired a variety of modalities according to varying circumstances, led to the increasing elimination of competition between the various territorial levels. States or departments as well as municipalities found themselves subjected to a progressive institutional weakening. The result was nothing less than a concentration of power in the political and institutional center, by which the provincial periphery, on the one hand, and the general public, on the other, were stripped of any possibility of participating in public affairs. Centralism came to represent the most significant characteristic of the Latin American state, which thereby acquired authoritarian tendencies capable of subduing the democratic spirit of many government officials.

During the course of democratic development, the role of political parties is of course significant. However, the meager development of civil society and statist centralism generated a tension that led to the deformation of the party function. The parties, especially the most important ones, found themselves compelled to join the state structure in order to obtain that which the weak civil society could not obtain directly. This orientation has given political parties an increasing identification with the state and united them as a privileged element of its apparatus.

The most direct consequence of all of this has been the development of a client-oriented style of politics. The power of the parties comes increasingly from their ability to trade positions and sinecures in exchange for political support. This has perverted not only the parties, but also the state. The public apparatus is increasingly a territory colonized by clientele-based demands, with a subsequent and permanent decapitalization of the human factor as a result of the pressure of political-partisan fluctuations.

The gelatinous character of the state is most directly expressed in the absence or loss of institutionality. Power does not lie where the constitution and the laws dictate, but rather in elements—frequently partisan in nature—that undermine and dominate it. Strictly speaking, it is not the Congress that legislates; it is not the judicial branch that guarantees lawfulness. This condition of profoundly weakened institutionality will have severe consequences for the very power of the state.

The repercussions of these dynamics are far reaching. Most importantly, we find that the Latin American state is extremely weak, in spite of its appearance of strength. To be sure, it is extensive and endowed with a quite broad capability for microsocial interference, but with regard to its real capability for effective intervention, direction, and regulation, the state is weak and fragile. State interventionism is not the ability to intervene in the Keynesian sense, with a capability to promote a strategic orientation of society. On the contrary, if there is one characteristic shared by all Latin American states, it is that they face a multitude of pressures of every type but often find it impossible to make strategic definitions. But this impasse does not keep the state, in its current condition, from overextending itself. It is broad, but weak; large, but flabby; omnipresent, but useless. These dynamics can be observed with considerable effort in the economy: The state has an invasive capability in the field of microeconomics, but lacks strength and ability for the macroeconomic management of society.

The state is constituted in this way because it is colonized by the interests of pressure groups and political parties, which parcel state power out among themselves. The state is an immense federation of resounding inefficiency, which generates tension in the general public and places further demands on the state. This pressure on the public sector and its inability to respond create the requisite conditions for the appearance of what we might call a "parallel state" of corruption, commissions, payoffs, and bribes, because it is by this route that one may achieve whatever is difficult or impossible via the institutional route. Corruption establishes its objective basis in this process, which, upon gaining social legitimacy, subsequently becomes a modality of primary accumulation for certain social sectors, especially those having close connections to the state, thus propitiating the corruption of many of the sectors linked with politics and of business transactions linked with public institutions.

Civil society is the eternal orphan in this framework. Civil society is often underdeveloped or at best only half developed, a condition that allows the state to permeate it decisively, to such an extent that society tends to be a state society. The citizen, in the deepest and most democratic sense of the word, as a social protagonist and focal point of rights and obligations, is nothing more than a legal fiction. He has been substituted by parastatal organizations that act in his behalf and that, in practice, exercise an authoritarian relationship with regard to society.

In this context, we must again refer to the political parties. They have been key pieces in the consolidation and development of democracy, but have been progressively modifying their role. Originally a creation and an expression of society—in most cases of the poorest layers of society—they eventually were joined to the state. Instead of being the voice of the street in the presence of the highest, they became the voice of the highest in the presence of the street. Only during election campaigns, the mechanism that legitimatizes their role in the state, do they recover their contact with the people in a fleeting and partial fashion. In this way they have developed an authorized relationship with society. To the extent to which the latter has matured—as a product, among other things, of the actual original democratic conduct of the parties—the demands on the parties become more acute and criticism more intense. Criticism is thus not antidemocratic in nature, but rather proof of the increasing invigoration of the general public in defense of its rights. This criticism comes not only from those not active in political parties, but increasingly from the members or adherents themselves, who tend to be privileged victims of the authoritarianism they themselves denounce.

This set of problems finds an answer in reform of the state, which is nothing more than another name for reform of society. It tends to be a modern response to the crisis, which does not consider democracy an obstacle but rather as a most powerful instrument with which to deal with the crisis. Reform implies legal changes, so as to modernize the legal mechanism of society; technological changes, to promote new forms of public government; and administrative changes, to produce the adjustments necessary in the public sector. But it is more than that. The reform of the state is largely a process of horizontal and vertical redistribution of power—horizontal in the sense that it spreads outward from the territorial centers toward the provinces; vertical in that it spreads outward from the nuclei in which power is concentrated toward the general public.

The reform of the state is the boldest project that the democratic systems of developing countries could ever have proposed for the radical modernization of society, especially in the framework of the crisis that overwhelms Latin American society today and the violent process of international transformations currently under way. This might well constitute the great Latin American project that will transport a modernized Latin America safely into the next century. It must be stressed that economic problems cannot be solved seriously and permanently outside the framework of an integral transformation of society and state.

The fundamental areas that need to be dealt with, from the perspective in which we have approached the problem, are as follows:

1. *Political reforms.* The purpose of this aspect of the project is to produce intense and growing participation by the general public, simultaneously promoting increased representativeness, by promoting a closer relationship between electors and the elected. It means modernizing the electoral system; reforming the mechanisms used by the parties for selecting their internal authorities and candidates for the various electoral offices; making the financial mechanisms of the political parties totally transparent; democratizing labor and professional movements; developing municipal power (in our case, the popular election of governors and mayors); and strengthening the values of democracy.

2. *Decentralization.* Decentralization unfolds in the political, administrative, and economic-financial fields. Its purpose is to promote democratization while decongesting the central level of the state in order to promote greater efficiency in its conduct. Decentralization implies a new era of territorial integration and a new way for the state to relate to the private citizen.

3. *Administrative modernization.* Public administration is a clear and condensed manifestation of the type of powers exercised in a society, both in its structure as well as in its functioning and policies with regard to personnel. In this perspective, it becomes essential to insist on the fundamental nuclei of the administrative process, stressing the professionalization of public administration as a decisive step toward banishing clientelism. Similarly, inroads must be made in the principal manifestation of the state vis-à-vis the general public—administrative procedures—in order to bring about their simplification.

4. *Modernization of the state of law.* A democracy cannot exist without a solid and reliable state of law. In periods of uncertainty, such as the current crisis, this need is even more urgent. It becomes the only mechanism for establishing clear and reliable rules of play. The reform of the judicial process, the modernization of the legislative function, the transformation of the penal-penitentiary system, the creation of mechanisms for defending private citizens against the violence of power—all constitute instruments of this transformation.

5. *Modernization of public policies.* How states conceive, decide, execute, control, and evaluate policies is part of our drama. We must begin a process of transformation for the development of public policies responding to the general interests of society. An example is the particular case of the relationship between economic and social policies, which often march toward different general objectives, the latter becoming the poor relation of the former, thus compromising the goals of the democratic state and social law.

6. *Development of civil society.* This implies making an effort to ensure that the various forms of expression and organization of society may flourish. It is not only a requirement of democracy, but an indispensable requirement for promoting the increased efficiency of the state. It is a matter of attempting to open the channels for developing a social power capable of taking the reforms and converting them into an irreversible and continuous process.

These elements constitute a strategy for the modernization of society, but such a process cannot be construed as a policy imposed from the top down, unrelated to the requirements and demands of society as a whole. Hence the need for permanent consultation and feedback in order to mobilize public opinion. This is not merely a way of promoting participation, but also of developing power capable of overcoming the opposition that is certain to surface eventually—since we are dealing with a process for redistributing power, for bringing down the privileged classes, and admitting the presence of emerging social forces.

6

Foreign Policy in Times of Change

Beatrice Rangel

As a result of its successful transition to democracy, Venezuela became a conspicuous foreign policy actor in the last fifteen to twenty years and felt that it should contribute to democratic order in the region. But Venezuelans are more concerned with internal party politics or baseball. Regardless of the outside perception of the Venezuelan role in world affairs, foreign policy in the democratic period has been the by-product of an intricate network of tradition and political realism resembling a description from Márquez's *One Hundred Years of Solitude*. Foreign policy has been the result of a desire to emulate the path taken by Simón Bolívar, regarded as the golden-age model in foreign affairs, and the need to create new channels of communication with other nations in the hemisphere as a result of the new openness of Venezuelan society.

Venezuela is taking into account the building blocks of any foreign policy—international environment, domestic environment, and the basic beliefs and guiding principles that inspire the leaders who formulate policy. In the 1950s, most of the surrounding countries were going through economic growing pains. Dictatorships abounded, controlling all but a few countries in the region. Venezuela and its leaders perceived this environment as a threat, and from 1958 to 1969, all foreign policy was formulated to modify this negative context, being diverted toward protecting and strengthening democracy. Foreign policy was thus subordinated to domestic policy goals dealing with stabilization.

From 1969 to about 1983, Venezuela was surrounded by expanding economies and the downfall of dictatorships, a renaissance of the spirit of independence and participation in the developing world and particularly Latin America. All foreign policy actions were directed toward promoting decolonization, strengthening democratic regimes being born elsewhere in Latin America, and increasing the use of resources to strengthen the negotiating capacity of these nations. This reflected a

Beatrice Rangel is former vice-minister of the Ministry of the Presidency of the Republic of Venezuela.

more future-oriented international context rather than one of isolationism.

The search for new economic and political viability started in 1984. We do not know how it is going to end. We now have political and economical crises threatening both the region and the internal politics of Venezuela. The Venezuelan elites are realizing that the country needs a new foreign policy geared toward the emergence of a new political space in Latin America and the promotion of a set of economic exchanges to foster domestic progress and solve the development crisis. As Minister Blanco very aptly put it, after thirty years of democracy, Venezuelans came to the realization that the system that had worked so well nevertheless had major pitfalls. Venezuelans wanted more participation and less control—less settlement of disputes by the elites and more participation of the different interest groups and intermediary organizations.

This search for a new political space is the result of research conducted by COPRE. This research basically dealt with two issues: governability in a changing international system, and the crisis of the nation-state. The dissatisfaction of Venezuelans with the shortcomings of the political system led to the conclusion that participatory democracy could only be obtained by new politically active groups.

The impact of this research was reinforced in the minds of foreign policymakers in Venezuela by two developments in the region that touched upon domestic issues. One of these was drug trafficking, regarded as destroying the essence of democracy and creating such by-products as crime and corruption. The second development was the persistence of the Central American conflict. Many of the processes that took place in Central America were also beginning to emerge or develop full-fledged in Colombia and Peru. Venezuelans felt they were being encircled by wars and subversion and that there was a need to act. The economic crisis prompted both the common man and the elite to search for a new strategy. For the first time, Venezuelans started looking to the external sector as a source of well-being since the major source of well-being—oil—seemed ineffective in providing the continued development and economic growth that Venezuela had known for forty years.

These developments prompted a foreign policy design geared toward strengthening political coordination among Latin American countries, in order to substitute for the growing inability of the nation-state to tackle international problems affecting internal political order. An objective of this new design is the development of a problem-solving approach to international economic relations. It tries to achieve a different pattern of relations with the United States, directed toward economic complementarity and political consultation—economic complementarity to extend the market and create a new source of growth, and political consultation to get the United States to participate in solving problems vital to Venezuelans, such as drug trafficking, the emergence of terrorism, and other subversive activities in the region. This pragmatic approach also aims to build a new economic unity that can support economic reform measures by enhancing the size of the market and fostering specialization among the nations of the Caribbean Basin. Most importantly, the new foreign policy design promises to fill the vacuum left by the state's withdrawal from some economic activities. This vacuum, now being filled with foreign investment, takes into consideration for the first time the role of the private sector.

Venezuela is marked by two main political groups advocating different approaches to foreign policy. One group, aware that factors in the external sector could make the system inviable, has developed a cautious attitude regarding Venezuelan activities abroad. For example, they tend to participate only in initiatives that they think are clearly designed to strengthen democratic institutions or provide economic benefit to Venezuela. The second group is an emerging elite seeing the external sector as a land of opportunities, and calling for a foreign policy structure as an essential political reform tool for Venezuela.

7

Commentary

Sally Shelton-Colby

Only a few decades ago, in the late 1950s and the early 1960s, Venezuelan democracy was not at all assured of success. During that period there was quite a significant insurgency in Venezuela. I did not have firsthand experience of Venezuela in those years, but I gather from those who did that there actually was some question as to whether democracy would survive. But today Venezuela is a good example of a country that has dealt effectively with a serious guerrilla insurgency while maintaining and continuing to strengthen democratic institutions and processes.

Minister Naím described a serious effort to reform the administrative structure of the Venezuelan government, further democratize and open up the system politically, and implement an impressive program of economic restructuring and opening, while pursuing an activist foreign policy. I cannot think of another country in the region that has promoted programs of political reform, administrative reform, economic reform, and an activist foreign policy all at the same time. Costa Rica may be a close second, but Costa Rica has not really been involved outside the Central American context to the extent that Venezuela has. So, the exuberance and energy of the president is still very much in evidence.

Beatrice Rangel emphasized that in many ways the promotion of democracy and human rights has been perhaps the most consistent thread throughout the last three decades of Venezuelan foreign policy. Now that elections have been achieved in most of Latin America, my hope for both Venezuela and my own government would be that we not stop there, but think about the next stage, which is just as important—the strengthening of democratic systems, institutions, and processes.

I am on the board of directors of the National Endowment for Democracy (NED). The US Congress has increased our budget by over 50 percent for programs in Eastern Europe. However, there are other large parts of the world, including Latin America, where political parties, independent businesses, and independent labor organizations still need strengthening.

Sally Shelton-Colby is professor of political science at Georgetown University.

Larry Diamond referred to Conciencia in Argentina, a group sponsored by NED. This group decided in 1984 that there was an urgent need to instruct Argentines, particularly the less-educated ones, about their rights and responsibilities in a democratic system. They developed a network reaching into the farthest corners of Argentine society, not just concentrating in Buenos Aires. That work has now been replicated in almost every country in South America that has gone through a political transition. These are the kinds of efforts that I would very much hope to see the US government, private groups, and perhaps those governments which, like that of Venezuela, have a strong commitment to democracy, engaging in the 1990s. We must not assume that as soon as a country has held an election, all of the problems have been solved.

US policy dialogue lacks a strong sense of the need for economic democracy. Essential to the process of strengthening democracy is the need to promote both economic growth and development. The US government has acknowledged the importance of policies that admit a resumption of growth; we also ought to be talking about policies to promote development. Indeed, the objective of growth ought to be to promote development.

Venezuela does not get the credit it deserves in Europe, Japan, and the United States for the economic reforms it has put into place. These reforms represent an enormously impressive program, perhaps unparalleled in any other Latin American country. Venezuela has been badly hurt, in terms of its image and climate for foreign investment, by the needed reform of the judicial system. It is absolutely essential that the process of making the judiciary truly independent should move forward. Investors must feel they have recourse through an independent judiciary before they will invest strongly in any given country.

There is also an interesting and important story to be told someday about the Venezuelan government's constructive efforts to find a workable political arrangement in Nicaragua, Panama, and Colombia. For the most part this has been done quietly, behind the scenes, and I think it is a good and long-overdue example of a Latin American government taking significant steps to help solve Latin America's problems.

President Carlos Salinas was in Washington recently to launch negotiations with President Bush that will someday lead to a free trade agreement (FTA) between Mexico and the United States. The Chileans are about to ask the US government to begin negotiations leading to an FTA. The Argentines are also about to request free trade negotiations and the same issue is probably on Brazil's agenda. Given the leadership President Carlos Andrés Pérez has demonstrated in terms of promoting political, administrative, and economic change, and his search for political settlements in a variety of regional conflicts, what might be the Venezuelan administration's possible future leadership role in some kind of new hemispheric economic regime, particularly regarding trade?

8

Discussion

Beatrice Rangel: The new hemispheric economic arrangement is one of the conditions seen as a fundamental target for Venezuelan foreign policy. We see this as a two-stage process. First, internal economic reform must be undertaken to make all the economies efficient, competitive, and so forth. The economies, particularly those of the weakest countries—which are the countries in the Caribbean Basin—must be made viable. They must also be made complementary because everyone wants access to the US market; and if everyone wants to sell potatoes in that market, then the Latin American economies will be competing among themselves. There must be some integration, specialization, development of services, and so on.

Second, the country can enter into an arrangement with the United States that will be more useful to all parties. We are trying to promote a new economic unity in the Caribbean Basin that can then be the basis for producing economic change. There is also a problem of scale. One cannot compare the potential of the Brazilian, Argentine, or Mexican markets to the potential of the Venezuelan market or that of any of the countries in Central America or the Caribbean.

Venezuelan Participant: If foreign policy is essential to Venezuelan development and not just complementary to policies in other sectors, then most of the internal changes in Venezuelan political and economic structure are not just generated internally, but also by external pressures that could be objective or just evaluated as such by our politicians. This is an important matter because we could raise a new question: To what extent is Venezuela's state reform a matter of external pressure and to what extent does it derive from internal demands?

Rangel: I do not think that any of the reforms are the product of external pressures. The Venezuelan political system reached a stage of exhaustion. The basic model of settling disputes and aggregating interest was exclusionary of the larger sectors of the society. Once there was rapid growth, modernization, and investments in education and health, people

111

became more informed; what they wanted next was to have political participation. For example, look at the process of reform in the electoral law and for electoral parties. This was a movement born in the grassroots; pressure was exerted from the bottom up. At the same time, looking at the external sector, the economic crisis produced these political reforms and allowed us to undertake economic reform. Therefore, I think they are complementary. I do not think pressure for change in Venezuela came from abroad into the domestic field.

Everett Bauman (El Nacional, *Caracas):* Before the last summit, the Russians brought in a large group of so-called experts to try to explain their political and economic problems. There seemed to be a great deal of confusion. The remark was made that the problem in Russia today is not that they do not have enough democracy, but that they do not have enough authority, that Gorbachev should have launched his economic reform when he first started out or, better still, that he should have held an election that would have given him legitimacy as president.

The two cases that have been cited here as examples of where considerable progress has been made are Chile and Mexico. In Chile, this was accomplished by a general with dictatorship. In Mexico, it was accomplished by President Carlos Salinas, who rules with the strong support of his party and with the apparent consent of the Mexican people, for the most part.

It seems to me there is a lack of political will in Venezuela. Minister Naím referred to the thirty-year myth of state populism as something that was finished. But the politicians do not seem to think that it is finished. Why does President Pérez, who used a lot of muscle in a cause that perhaps was not entirely popular, not use it to achieve more progress in Venezuela?

Rangel: I do not think there is a lack of political will, but the president, like any other political leader, has to yield to political realities. I do think the privatization project, which has been defined and adopted in cabinet, can be fully executed unless at least one political symbol is very cautiously circumvented—the latest anticorruption law. Because of the public debate that took place in enacting that law, it is seen as one of the shields that would prevent corruption in the public sector. Any government that tries to make substantial reforms in this law would be regarded with suspicion by the public. Thus, there has to be a process by which everybody understands the limitations this law puts on a privatization program before it is politically palatable to change the law.

Moreover, no one will buy the state-owned enterprises in the condition they are in right now. Minister Blanco described a process of taking over the structure of the Venezuelan state from the political parties.

Unions control the whole managerial process, making them very inefficient. There is the concern that labor problems will make these enterprises impossible to operate.

Sally Shelton-Colby: Foreign investors and Venezuela's creditors acknowledge and applaud the start Venezuela has made in reforming its economy. The measures that have been taken to control the money supply and fiscal policy are gigantic steps in the right direction.

Privatization does not happen easily or quickly. It is a long and difficult process to clean up companies so that one can then sell them. In Mexico, President de la Madrid simply shut down a number of inefficient small companies. Although he was elected in 1982, he really was not able to start privatizing until about 1985–1986. In fact, some of the really big state-owned companies in Mexico are only just now being put up for privatization. Although there are still some remaining steps that need to be taken in terms of phasing out subsidies to state-owned enterprises and the start of a privitization process, Venezuela has nevertheless made a start that is being recognized by foreign investors.

Edwin Corr (University of Oklahoma): All of us rejoice in the achievements of democracy and the attention being given to democracy. It is popular today to say that socialism is dead, that the free market is the greatest generator of growth, and that we have to have economic growth if democracy is going to survive.

Taking into account the two-and-a-half decades of rather remarkable growth in Latin America from the late 1950s to the 1970s, what was popularly called the "trickle down" did not work too well. Given the liberal approach to the economy, the desire to let the market operate and generate wealth, what specific programs and policies do you envision to bring about a more equitable distribution of wealth within the society?

Rangel: There are at least two ways that we might deal with income distribution. One is decentralization. We should reform the national tax law to allow communities to create the resource base to finance their services, manage them, and supervise their quality. A second area that I think has a future is that of microenterprises. The Institute of Foreign Trade has a program that trains people to assemble products for export. There is also a pilot project in one of the Venezuelan states, known for producing oil, that also has a rich agriculture zone. Aided by this state microenterprise program, entrepreneurs and peasants have rallied together to form cooperatives to export tropical fruits to Europe. As a result of decentralization and programs such as these there will be a better distribution of income in Venezuela in the future.

Douglas Chalmers (Columbia University): Mexico seems to have turned away from Latin America in the direction of the United States, since opportunities for development would probably lie there, not in Colombia and Peru. So one could argue that the long-term trend is going to make the Venezuelan initiative an exception rather than the rule. But Sally Shelton complimented your country on your activities as Latin Americans seeking or providing assistance to solve the region's problems. Is this founded on a long-term process that is going to be solidified, or is it the product of the enthusiasm and energy of your president?

Rangel: The current Venezuelan activities in conflict resolution in Central America are a by-product of a long-standing foreign policy of intervening positively in Latin American affairs so as to strengthen democratic institutions and create the conditions for peace. President Pérez was not in power when that initiative took place, but he has added the extra element of his own personality and strong convictions.

The governments of the Caribbean Basin are having to deal with international problems such as drug trafficking and the economic crisis. In order for them ultimately to have a more fruitful relationship with the largest economy in the hemisphere, the US economy, we must work on creating the political and economic conditions for development to take place. Therefore, I think Venezuela will continue with this foreign policy line. This attitude of positive intervention and exploiting new opportunities abroad in order to promote welfare and better economic conditions among the countries in the Caribbean Basin may be a Venezuelan idiosyncrasy.

Venezuelan Participant: Venezuelan influence in the international arena may well have a great deal to do with its character as a self-identified and externally identified democratic, positively interventionist power. This character provides leverage in the international system and may or may not provide added political space domestically. What is your estimate of the domestic political ramifications of this positively interventionist policy?

Also, Venezuela's policy to be positively interventionist clearly must affect the United States. The Eisenhower administration's approach suffered two-and-a-half years of political frustration. Then Kennedy assumed the presidency and started to use this initiative not just for Latin American or Venezuelan purposes, but also for US purposes. What is your impression of the US reaction to Venezuela's intervention?

Rangel: When Venezuelans take an interest in foreign policy, they try to resolve a conflict or find the solution to a problem, rather than just be a bystander. No one criticizes conflict resolution initiatives by the government as long as they do not cost money. Social programs are being cut, subsidies are being suspended, and there is a scarcity of resources for many development programs; the government says it must ask the World Bank or the Inter-American Development Bank to lend them the money, for instance, to build a bridge or to continue to develop the railroad system. People ask how, at the same time, could Venezuela give any credits to the Central American and Caribbean nations?

As for relations with the United States, even though we agree on the goals, I think that there are many differences in views, approaches, and procedures—mostly cultural and informational differences. Foreign policy in the United States is part of the domestic rivalries between the government and the opposition, Congress and the White House. When so many actors with hidden agendas that are largely domestic in nature are involved with foreign policy, as is the case in the United States, then differences in perceptions and approaches develop, even though there is agreement between the two countries on the goals being pursued.

President Pérez says one of the miracles performed by the Reagan administration was that it kept the Sandinista leadership together for ten years, that foreign aggression created the conditions for people who were intrinisically different to rally together. This prevented the development of competition among themselves for leadership within the Nicaraguan government and altered the conditions for change within the country. So, although there was agreement between the United States and Venezuela that there had to be democracy in Nicaragua, the approach and the instruments used by the two countries were totally different.

PART 4

VENEZUELAN POLITICS AND POLICYMAKING

9

An Evaluation of the First Year of the Government of Carlos Andrés Peréz

Andrés Stambouli

On February 2, 1989, Carlos Andrés Pérez took office for the second time as president of the republic. During the electoral campaign, his public relations messages and those of his principal opponent, Eduardo Fernández of the COPEI (Social Christian party), did not reveal the contents of their respective public policy programs, which were to be implemented once they took office. The administration of President Lusinchi was not a campaign issue for the opposition; it received a favorable evaluation by public opinion, as reflected in the polls, as a result of astute handling of government policy with regard to information and public relations. The campaign strategy of Eduardo Fernández aimed to present the antecedents of the cases of corruption in which former President Pérez was once involved and subsequently to warn of supposed stands taken by Pérez that were unfavorable to Venezuelan interests in its border dispute with Colombia. The Pérez campaign, for all practical purposes, replicated the same campaign that produced his victory in 1974; optimism and veiled messianism were its chief elements. For many people, the return of Carlos Andrés as president meant the return of the prosperous times of his first administration. For others, it meant the danger of the reissuance of a plan, contemptuously called "populist," which was totally inappropriate for the current situation. The truth is that nothing was known with any reasonable certainty about the intentions of Carlos Andrés Pérez or of his principal opponent with regard to their proposed formula of government.

But for anyone who had read the government programs of both candidates—and very few voters had done so—the similarities in the offerings stood out: less of a state role, more market mechanisms, privatization, decentralizing political reforms, export-oriented economy, and so forth. The problem was that neither candidate elaborated on the magnitude of the economic problems their programs were based on, problems that would subsequently be revealed in all their intensity. The

Andrés Stambouli is a private consultant and former advisor to the Presidential Commission for State Reform of the Republic of Venezuela.

general public was unaware of the seriousness of the situation, wrapped up as it was in believing the government would deliver a sound Venezuela to the successor.

The country had not yet gotten over the festive atmosphere surrounding the inauguration when, on February 14, President Pérez removed the veil to reveal enormous imbalances and economic shortages. He announced the Adjustment Plan, a series of economic measures that took the country by surprise. Thirteen days later, the most terrible acts of social violence ever seen in the republican history of Venezuela erupted. Once the events were under control, and before the very eyes of a society that had not yet gotten over its bewilderment and astonishment, there was unleashed the most severe opposition against its economic policy ever experienced by any democratic government in Venezuela, an opposition that still exists, though somewhat more restrained. The business community, labor unions, opposition political parties, and even a portion of the governing party itself took on the task of actively importuning the administration to abandon its "economic package." The government insistently reiterated its objectives while responding that its critics had presented no alternatives for dealing with this serious situation.

After more than a year of government, the economic program of the Pérez administration was imposed. Eduardo Fernández, currently secretary-general of COPEI, recognizes the value and need for the macroeconomic measures, though he denounces the lack of coherence in the governmental team and the lack of depth in those measures that are complementary to the plan, such as the policy of privatization. The National Industrial Board warns of the dangers that could be set in motion by a reversal of economic policy. The Venezuelan Workers Confederation acknowledged the irreversible nature of the current socioeconomic direction. Within the government party, Acción Democrática, important leaders have publicly recognized the inevitability and obligatory nature of the economic policies that were adopted. At the present time, the public debate over government policy is focused on the announced increase in the price of gasoline, though those opposing the measure do not challenge the entire package of economic policies.

During thirty-two years of democratic government, Venezuelans developed a culture for agreeing with the public policies of the state without lengthy debate. In effect, the structure that linked the bureaucratic apparatus of the state with the political parties, interest groups, and influential individuals was based, by virtue of the situation of relative abundance, on a non–zero sum game. That fact produced the operating conditions of a stable democracy while generating a situation of economic inefficiency, clientelism, corruption, and social participation mediated by the political parties.

Thus, the successive administrations lacked true programs of sectoral action. The candidates, while on the campaign trail, tended to introduce as their programs some very generous and ambiguous formulations as the goals of their government. In turn, those governing, along with the various branches of the executive power, included the demands made on them by their various clienteles when preparing their sectoral action plans. The best choice became not the plan that was better constructed from the technical and programmatic point of view, but rather the one with the greatest support. Thus, governing consisted less in the application of an action program and more in the ability to serve and satisfy those individuals, groups, and clientele having linkages to one or another government ministry. Political rationality, a product of the deliberate attempt to reduce conflicts and controversies, predominated over programmatic rationality.

This modality of government and decisionmaking generated customs and expectations impeding progress toward the exercise of executive power at the national level based on real-world programmatic rationality, an approach that the government of President Pérez began to introduce. This programmatic approach required the practice of negotiation, virtually unknown to the Venezuela of recent decades. Indeed, resistance and opposition to the application of the economic package by various sectors of society, and in particular by some of the leading figures of the governing party itself, are not so much the result of the specific nature of that program, but rather of the very fact that it does indeed represent a program that tends to water down the benefits provided by preceding administrations to the governing parties and those sectors involved in policy formulation. Thus, a new political game has begun in Venezuela: a debate over controversial public policies aimed at a more market-oriented economy in a society long unaccustomed to debating, thanks to state intervention, regulation, protection, and subsidies.

Another novel game beginning today is the decentralization of political, party, and governmental structures and institutions, which will also require training in political negotiation. It is becoming increasingly difficult to impose policy decisions from the center outward toward the periphery, even when a policy seems indisputable. The president must negotiate with popularly elected state governors and the central structures of the political parties must pay greater attention to regional organizations and leaders, as well as to cases of internal dissent regarding the positions assumed with respect to government policies. The political game has become more pluralistic and more autonomous. It is not unusual to find opposition leaders supporting the government and government party leaders opposing it. This change of direction from a centralized populist democratic system to one in which the political and economic market is more vigorous constitutes the central challenge not only for Venezuela but for all of Latin America. The pessimistic interpretation of Latin American politics, according to which we had to choose between populist democracy and authoritarianism, is being refuted. Indeed, in current practice democratic regimes are waging the battle against populism—with considerable difficulty, to be sure, but with good prospects for success.

The first year of the government of Carlos Andrés Pérez has meant transition from a country whose social peace was sustained through petroleum-based financing to the building of a political culture of controversy, debate, negotiation, and institutionally motivated conflict, not to be confused with crisis, chaos, or dissolution. Venezuela finds itself in a process of restructuring the orientation of its social, economic and, above all, political interactions.

Past experience shows that an important source of government ineffectiveness was the failure to form ministerial teams joined by a shared programmatic platform. To a very important degree, previous governments lacked programs that could logically precede the formulation of sectoral policies. In selecting his economic team, President Pérez responded less to the traditional criteria of rewarding political collaborators or friends and more to the criteria of technopolitical competence required for the formulation and implementation of policies to adequately support the program. Only a team of this type could initiate the necessary transition from the political rationality of consensus for sharing to the programmatic rationality for instrumental efficiency.

But this arrangement became a major source of difficulties for the government. In effect, the political opposition as well as several social sectors reproached the government for presenting a prefabricated program with no allowance for modifications of substance. In effect, what these sectors wanted was for each and every one of their petitions to be welcomed in accordance with the established custom of policy formulation. The new approach signified a drastic change both in the content of economic policies as well as in the style of the decisionmaking process. This sudden change in direction against a background of thirty years of inertia was a source of bewilderment for society. The acceptance of scarcity as an immutable fact over the short and medium term, as well as the understanding of the consequences thereof, is no small task; certain sectors demanded a return to the times when a dollar could be purchased for 4.30 bolivars.

Acción Democrática is undergoing internal disturbances, tensions, and confrontations produced not only by the struggle for control over the party machinery by leaders who have stood face to face for several years, but also as a consequence of its role as governing party, affected by the decisions taken by President Pérez with regard to supporters and economic policy. Some high-ranking authorities of the party have complained that Acción Democrática is in some ways a government party and in other ways is not. Two-thirds of the ministerial cabinet consists of individuals not belonging to the party, severely constraining the privileged access to the government customarily enjoyed by the party. Some noted leaders of Acción Democrática have even complained openly of not being able to place a party colleague as a doorperson in a ministry building.

In addition, the announcement of the restructuring and privatization of certain public sector enterprises, with the implication of a significant reduction in the capability of the party to dole out favors to its clientele, worries certain party chieftains who see in it a major erosion of their sources of power. It is also worth noting the complaint of the secretary-general of the party with regard to the reorganization, supposedly without the benefit of consultation with the party, of the Ministry of Development, with clear references to the reduced numbers of militant party members in public posts.

If we add to this the December 1989 election losses by party candidates in the gubernatorial races in the most important states of the country—Miranda, Aragua, Carabobo, Zulia, and Bolívar, in addition to Anzoátegui, Mérida and Yaracuy—it is easy to understand the concern of the party directorship faced with an upcoming convention in which new party leaders are to be elected. In these circumstances, criticism of the government and its economic package appear to be inspired from within the party as a result of the internal struggle to maintain control of the party machinery.

The government has permanently ratified the basic premises of its economic program and new decisions for strengthening it are constantly being produced or analyzed. That program has significant support and backing at the national and international levels. Within both the government party and the principal opposition party, as well as in other minority parties, there have been public demonstrations in favor of the program's fundamental concepts. Important business and executive groups have also given their support to the new policy aimed at a competitive market economy. There is no reason to believe that the economic and political program of the government might be reversed or substantially modified. The president evidently values national and international support for his government administration more than the demands of a given sector of his party.

Along another line of thinking, the phantom of "February 27, 1989" is on the minds of officials at the policy- and decisionmaking levels. The government, political parties, and state security organizations are now more sensitized and alert to a potential social explosion. Accordingly, policy decisions relating to the program continue to be considered, though now they are carefully measured and better prepared. Every effort is made to create a climate of consensus for the most controversial of these decisions, such as increases in the domestic price of gasoline.

If there is anything to be gleaned from this first year of government by President Pérez, it is that communications between the government and society have changed significantly in both form and content as far as the government decisionmaking process is concerned. Venezuelan society is thereby demonstrating that its democracy, far from being petrified, has a considerable capacity for adapting to changing times.

Venezuela is eliminating the need to resort to an authoritarian-type regime by broadening the democratic regime through decentralization, and perfecting its representative capability. In doing so, it is demonstrating that clientele-based populism is not the only way to live democratically in Latin America, as certain pessimistic and even disparaging theories would have it. The most recent events in which the popular will has been manifested—the municipal and state elections of December 1989—proved that the citizens of Venezuela know how to use their vote to express both their displeasure and their approval. The protective democracy born in the early seventies has today become a mature democracy. In all certainty, the origin of the changes in the beginning of the 1990s in the form of governing, in how the opposition operates, and in how the general public expresses itself augurs well for positive and even more profound changes in the quality of Venezuelan democracy over the medium term.

Most certainly the quality of political debate will improve, becoming increasingly program-oriented. In this sense, for example, the political leadership will attempt to lay the foundations of legitimacy through its substantive policy decisions and actions, rather than just through the public image it projects. No doubt the political parties will now be collectively more attuned to the platforms proposed by their candidates, so that neither they nor the voters will be taken by surprise. Government policies will thus be able to count on a reserve of democratic legitimacy for which there is no substitute: voter support for government action. Meanwhile, the Venezuelan political system is assisting in the exorcism of the old way of doing politics, which was more of a bureaucratic struggle for positions of power than a discussion of the appropriate government agenda for dealing with the problems of the country.

10

Opposition in Times of Change

Gustavo Tarre Briceño

Western political tradition, as it refers to representative democracies, created a culture and practice in which, once the popular will has been expressed, the majority governs and the minority not only respects the outcome but also assumes the institutional and constitutional role of opposition. Between one election and the next, the private citizen analyzes government policies in the light of criticisms presented by the opposition. This process will later translate into a new electoral decision.

In stable democracies and normal times, government and opposition activities are carried out without incident. Parliamentary dynamics, despite the harshness sometimes observed in political debate, allows points of convergence or concurrence to be reached. In times of crisis, the debate may become radicalized and opposition may become an obstruction; or, on the contrary, the convergence may actually be accentuated. There are no preestablished recipes. Thus, we find British war cabinets integrated by both parties; French cohabitation; institutional convergence in Colombia; bipartisan politics in the United States, and every variety of governmental pacts, agreements, and coalitions.

Until 1958, opposition in Venezuela manifested itself largely through the use of arms. Power was achieved on the basis of victorious revolutions, although that is not to suggest the existence of civic opposition during the few lapses into parliamentary life. The press was the oppositional tribunal par excellence when the guns were silent. But it was never a reasonable opposition. The fundamental goal was always destruction of the government.

On the fall of the dictatorship of General Marcos Pérez Jiménez, the three principal parties—of opposing ideological tendencies—signed the so-called *Pacto de Punto Fijo* (literally, the Fixed-Point Pact). On the basis of this agreement, the political system was able to achieve stability through a government coalition of the most important of the political forces that participated in the elections of December 1958. In the decade

Gustavo Tarre Briceño is parliamentary leader of the Social Christian party of Venezuela (COPEI).

that followed, forms of democratic opposition coexisted in the media and in parliament, along with anachronistic forms of traditional militarism and new expressions of Marxist guerrillas. During the presidency of Rafael Caldera, the country was finally pacified and the opposition moved exclusively along democratic channels. During the first fifteen years of the current political system, certain goals were achieved that in some countries are normal but which were quite novel in Venezuela. In 1964, for the first time, a president elected by the people handed over power to another president elected by the people. In 1969, also for the first time, a president of one political party handed over power to another president of a different political party. Alternation became quite normal and nobody today would deny that the opposition can ascend to power by peaceful means and in a climate of respect for individual liberties. The consensus was built around a constitutional, political, social, and economic scheme.

After thirty-two years of democratic governments, people became tired of the model. The various styles of political relationships (of the governing powers vis-à-vis the people) and concepts of the state were exhausted. The political parties ceased to be drive belts between the citizens and the public institutions. The representative entities maintained few links with the electors. The electoral system excessively favored the political parties, to the detriment of the individual. Thus was created the famous paradox, denounced by Raymond Carré de Malberg, by virtue of which "the representative does not represent the represented."

Statism and populism were unable to endure the economic crisis unleashed by the drop in petroleum prices and burgeoning external debt. This was the historical collapse of populism, understood in the case of Venezuela as a particular way of articulating political action with regard to popular demands, on the basis of the automatic and increasing satisfaction of social requirements by redistribution of oil income. Statism—that is, the excessive and precipitous presence of the public sector in all facets of economic and social life—was found wanting.

The Venezuelan state undertakes many and diverse activities, all inefficiently. It becomes involved in communications, postal service, telephone service, and mass transportation; it manages heavy industry and large hotels; it assumes ownership of banks and airlines; it provides all public services, including education, at all levels. The omnipresent state, not for that reason any stronger, is an inefficient giant reminiscent of the "philanthropic ogre" described by Octavio Paz.

The long crisis is daily present in Venezuelan reality. In the street, one can sense the protests of the poor, the outcasts, the unemployed. One can also sense the anguish of the middle class, caught up in the process of becoming proletarianized. One can sense the deterioration of the quality of life, the inflation that is destroying the purchasing power of all Venezuelans, the growing delinquency ignored by the police force. One can sense the corruption, no longer a mild symptom but an expanding force in a society without strong values. One can sense an inefficient judicial system, sometimes corrupt and always slow, and the loss of faith in the leaders and political parties, seen more as communities of vested interests than of convictions.

Consensus and legitimacy are blood relatives. Legitimate power is, among other things, that which effectively carries out the community-service missions that justify its existence. If the community feels that these missions are not being carried out, the consensus—that desire to live and be together, which, no matter how passive, is what allows society to progress and maintain its stability—is lost. Thus, all that remains is the resort to force, but force alone is incapable of guaranteeing community life. When faced by a general refusal to accept the rules of the game, repression is overwhelmed by the masses. The events of February 27 and 28, 1989, were a clear and alarming expression of a consensus which may be crumbling: three hundred officially listed as dead, thousands wounded, the army in the streets, and civil power completely inhibited. Ten months later, the discontent once again manifested itself in a spectacular fashion: in the election for governors, mayors, and city councilmen, abstention reached 55 percent, something absolutely unheard of in a country accustomed to extremely high electoral turnouts. The polls carried out following the elections showed that the abstention was due largely to distrust and skepticism.

In the electoral campaign of 1988, the presidential candidate of COPEI, Eduardo Fernández, used the slogan "The Change." Today, the administration of President Carlos Andrés Pérez has announced a "Great Turnaround." The need for change is felt everywhere. Antonio Gramsci used to say that "the crisis consists precisely in the fact that the old dies and the new is unable to be born." Venezuela needs change and a turnaround so that a new consensus might be born.

In this sense, we have taken important steps, albeit only initial ones, which are leaving their imprint on recent democratic developments in Venezuela and will have greater impact in the immediate future as well as over the long term. Among these achievements we must note the popular election of mayors and governors, the transfer of power from the nation to the states, and the modifications made to the electoral system. This marks the beginning of deconcentration of political power and reduction in the "infra-representativeness" blighting the effectiveness, administrative capability, and credibility of partisan leadership, and which involves a reduction of the excessive weight of central power in subordinate-level decisions in public administration and political power— including decisions at the grassroots level relating directly to the individual citizen. Consider that up until last year, state governors were named by the president at his discretion, cities did not have mayors, and one would vote by placing a mark on colored cards in order to simultaneously elect state and national legislators.

There is a growing effort aimed at the reduction of the state apparatus, an effort born from within. The initiative has been taken by the political parties, notwithstanding the resistance encountered therein. That is to say, the initiative originates in those who were frequently accused of being incompatible adversaries of the process by which statism and favoritism were weakened. We are dealing with a process that has profound cultural implications, not only for habits of the general public, but also, and most importantly, for the culture of political leadership, the style of relationships habitually established between governing and opposition forces, and the dynamics governing the relationship between government and government party. The unanswered question has to do with the timeliness and degree of intensity of the change.

It is an inarguable fact that, from the perspective of constitutional theory, the government derives a good deal of its legitimacy from the majority will of the voters, freely expressed through the mechanism of suffrage. Whoever receives the favor of the people in democratic elections—at least in elections held in the democratic style of the Western world—consents to assume political power and implement a government action program, which, whether in practice or in theory, is supported by the voter.

By definition, the government governs and the opposition opposes. This concept is not totally accepted today by public opinion in Venezuela. The country becomes impassioned during the electoral campaign, but it is hoped that everyone will support the new government of Venezuela once the campaign is concluded. The party militants who were not favored by the election results, in contrast, aspire to radical opposition. Both extremes are bad.

There has to be opposition; it forms an essential part of the democratic dialectic. The people, as electors, must analyze government policies in the light of criticisms expressed by the opposition. This entire process leads to the formation of a will that is later translated into an electoral decision. But that opposition cannot be given free rein: It cannot attack the vital interests of the country. Where is the point of equilibrium? Leon Blum, council president in the French Popular Front, used to say that the opposition parties could not oppose those government measures that they would have implemented in the exact same way had they themselves won the elections. This appears to be a good criterion. It supposes, in addition, that the government-opposition confrontation should not be a struggle to the death. The opposition does not seek to impede government action, much less destroy the government. The latter cannot pretend to silence the opposition or stop it from acting. Georges Burdeau states that the power and the opposition form what, in mechanics, is called a system and that energy—in this case political energy—is produced not by unilateral force but by a resultant force derived from the forces generated by the system. It is not a "zero sum" game in which the gain of one is achieved wholly at the expense of the other. The sole winner must be the general public as a whole.

In addition, it is necessary to establish understandings for the long term. In systems where government control alternates between political parties, there are some policies that must remain in place for several administrations. If we observe those countries that have managed to escape underdevelopment, there is one clear constant: long-term plans, policies developed over a period of twenty years, allowed Japan, South Korea, Taiwan, and Singapore to become industrial powers. Our long-term policies in petroleum, education, defense, and exports, for example, cannot be subjected to political circumstance. Agreements are also required over the short term: there should be no marked differences on issues of foreign policy or foreign debt. The general trend for the opposition is provided by the government.

All the above suggests that the government should call upon the opposition to assist in the design of policies and not limit itself to presenting "contracts of adherence" that the opposing parties must either take or leave. Such a procedure is not yet part of Venezuelan political culture. The government desires support, considering any dissidence unpatriotic. The militant members of the opposition see in this coming together something very close to surrender or treason. The British idea of a loyal opposition has not penetrated into our practice, nor is it generally understood. Certain facts, however, compel us to conceive a different opposition:

1. The government does not have a parliamentary majority. Consequently, all decisions require agreements and negotiations.
2. The opposition holds nine of the twenty governorships, including those of the majority of the most important and most densely populated states, as well as almost half of the mayoralties. The responsibility for administration is no longer the exclusive realm of the central authority. The opposition *is* the government in half of the country. This reality, perfectly assimilated in the United States, is totally new for us.
3. Some of the measures taken by the government, such as unification of the exchange rate, floating of interest rates, suppression of tariff protections, industrial reconversion, elimination of certain subsidies—all had to be made by any serious government that

would have taken the reins of the country in 1988. The errors committed by the Pérez government have nothing to do with the diagnosis nor with the general outlines provided. The government made mistakes with regard to the timing of the measures, in the degree of intensity and implementation of those measures, and in the social compensation offered.

The preceding does not suggest that the central administration lacks responsibility and that it is not wise to point them out and denounce the errors of the government. There are serious structural flaws:

1. The reduction in the size of the state forms a part of government rhetoric but not of government practice. Public expenditures have decreased with regard to investments, but not with regard to the bureaucracy and expenditures on luxury items. Privatization has not yet begun. After a period of fifteen months, President Salinas de Gortari has privatized two hundred enterprises in Mexico. In the same time period, the Venezuelan government has not privatized any.
2. Nothing has been done to implement a merit system in public administration. Government functionaries continue to be tapped on the basis of party affiliation, family connections, or friendships.
3. The struggle against corruption, an essential part of the government discourse, is a myth. The *Report of the Controller General of the Republic* for 1989 illustrates not only that has corruption not decreased, but that it has actually increased. The government has done very little to facilitate the punishment of those who obtained illicit wealth during the administration of Jaime Lusinchi.

If to these flaws we add the circumstantial errors, there is a great deal of room for opposition. The latter must also present alternatives. It should say to the country: This is what we would have done if we were governing the country, or this is what we will do when we win the coming elections. In addition, a qualitative change must take place. In exchange for the votes the government needs in parliament for the approval of its projects, the opposition may set as a condition the government's approval of its ideas.

Times of change demand a change in opposition. We must educate in order to change people's ways of thinking. We hope leaders will not surface in the political parties who find in the demagoguery of a radical opposition a political space to provide them with personal gain. We hope the government will understand that to heed the call of the opposition does not in the least impair the principle of authority, but rather dignifies it. Difficulties demand understandings. It is up to the government to design the scenarios that will allow such understanding. An agreement of wills is required, one that includes the political parties, labor unions, business organizations, and government. The "agreement" up until now has been mere government propaganda. We can make it a reality, if such is the will of the government. In this way, we can begin to build a new consensus.

11

Commentary

John D. Martz

The centrality of political parties in Venezuela is obvious. For a comparative study of the developing world or of Latin American politics for processes of democratization over a period of years, Venezuela is the best case. For all its strengths and weaknesses, it is an exciting and stimulating country. I once argued that Venezuelan political parties were in danger of petrification. Perhaps a somewhat better term would be malaise, a poor condition of health that is obviously not terminal. It suggests that there are remedies, treatments, and that the problems that may be serious can be dealt with and mitigated. It is useful to remember that there are a number of broad capacities for change and adaptation; the Venezuelan political system has vitality and flexibility.

In 1958 there were essentially four parties—three sizable and substantial ones, and the quite small Communist party. Over the following ten to fifteen years, there was even a proliferation of political parties and the evolution of what seemed an increasingly fragmented multiparty system. We added to that the occasional electoral phenomenon, particularly in Caracas, every five years. Suddenly, in 1973, Venezuela held the critical election in which, despite the participation of twelve presidential candidates that year, AD and COPEI emerged as the dominant actors in the party system, which of course they continue to maintain at the present time.

Remember, going back to 1964 at the outset of the Leoni administration, the Leoni government and some opposition parties including COPEI chose not to enter formally into a government coalition. There was a constructive opposition, an element of which is certainly maintained in Venezuelan politics today. To be sure, it was easier in times of relative affluence to agree to disagree, to maintain a system in which there was often very little formal debate or dialogue in Congress, and little give and take in terms of negotiation. Still, this was in many ways the strength of the Venezuelan party system. Civility and ultimate consensus between leaders of rival political parties in terms of national goals

John D. Martz is professor of political science at Pennsylvania State University.

and national welfare is accepted in the Venezuelan political system to a degree not found in many other countries in the developing world or even beyond. This capacity to cooperate, to collaborate, is now about to take new forms in Venezuela as we enter the decade of the 1990s.

We have also seen that from time to time, despite bouts of petrification in the party system, there has also been a willingness to respond. Certainly it has been true, for example, that an outgoing president has not been able to name his handpicked successor in the political party. There have been occasions when the electoral preferences of those who presumably control the party apparatus found that their electoral preferences did not necessarily reach the mass of the party. We had an example of this with the last nomination of now President Pérez. Essentially he appealed to the mass of the party and won the nomination.

One can perhaps exaggerate the depth of public dissatisfaction with Venezuela's party system. On the other hand, one can argue that, given the nature of the socioeconomic pressures under which most Venezuelans live and the comparatively much more comfortable lives they were long accustomed to, there will inevitably be dissatisfaction and unhappiness. Given the nature of the Venezuelan system, where will that sentiment be directed?

In terms of some of the reforms of the political parties and party laws, certainly there are strong pressures for change from outside the parties. The political party leaders are not unaware of these; after all, some have been advocating such changes for several years. Others have felt that they should change, but were uneasy about whether the time was appropriate. But it is possible to be unduly critical of rigidity in leaders of the party central committees, for example, and other high-ranking members of the party hierarchy. Some of the changes are going to come from inside the party. To the extent that this is possible, such changes are likely to be healthier than those mandated by Congress.

There were times in his campaign when Pérez tried to claim that things are different than they were in the 1970s, that the public should not assume that everything was going to be the same as when he was president the first time. But that assumption was natural. Venezuelans were asked in public opinion polls after the Pérez election whether they thought the situation would get better in the next six months and in the next five years. In both cases, the outlook was optimistic. Clearly they felt things had not been going well, but now that President Pérez was back, somehow everything was going to improve in a relatively short period of time. This expectation placed a burden on the Pérez government, and such hopes certainly would have been a burden for Fernández had he been elected. The expectations were unrealistic, as was reflected in part in the nature of the campaign that had dominated the efforts of both candidates.

Those of us familiar with Latin America in general and those of us who are comparativists, looking at the accomplishments and the strengths, as well as the weaknesses, of the party system, find a rather remarkably positive experience in Venezuela, as contrasted with that of many of its neighbors. But today we are also at an historically important juncture in the evolution of Venezuelan politics. Clearly we had one in 1958–1959. Years have passed; Venezuelan society has changed; the world has changed; party leaders and all Venezuelans have much to learn and are in the process of learning. This, too, has broad applicability elsewhere in Latin America. Andrés Stambouli talks about populist democracy and the decline or failures of the populist model in Latin America, which we see increasingly in a number of other countries in the region. This represents an attempt to change or move away from the kind of classic state centralization that has been so crucial to governing and to the role of the state in Latin America, and certainly Venezuela.

So one sees the failures and weakening of the populist approach in Latin America generally and the inevitable and very important shift away from the emphasis on centralization and political patronage. This shift helps to delineate the beginning of a truly new era in Venezuela, an era that was destined to occur regardless which party prevailed in the last elections.

Notwithstanding the many problems plaguing the political parties, the need for reform, and the need for change in a variety of customs, there is a demonstrated capacity on the part of the political parties and party elites in Venezuela to respond—in some cases reluctantly, in other cases willingly. The response is under way, and ultimately we will see a renewed and somewhat different political system, one in which the parties will still play a central role.

12

Commentary

Diego Abente

Venezuela is taking a serious initiative. Carlos Andrés Pérez, in his second administration, is in fact inaugurating or at least seeking to inaugurate a new style of doing politics. The old style is characterized by clientelism, inefficiency, corruption, party-mediated social participation, and a non-programmatic approach to politics. In contrast, under Pérez we have a new administration and a new programmatic approach. Of course there is a lot of vested interest within the Venezuelan political system, party, state, and bureaucracy—a vast network opposed to these changes. But the changes are going forward nonetheless.

In the first Pérez administration in the 1970s, just about every major political, economic, or social decision was adopted after broad consultations with a number of important interest groups, particularly in business and labor. What we see now is a thoroughly different style of decisionmaking, relying more heavily on a group of advisors and in some ways trying to insulate the government from the pressure of precisely the same actors who played such a significant role in his first administration.

This raises the question of how to move in the direction of change, greater efficiency, and profound restructuring without sacrificing a democratic and participatory decisionmaking style. The change from the old style of doing politics to the present mode of operation has reflected a change from a strong party-link constituency and, therefore, a structure of accountability geared toward satisfying this clientele, to a much broader, societywide constituency, which is of course generating a different kind of pressure—different demands with different expectations for their fulfillment by the government. Overall, this shift reflects the process of modernization of Venezuelan society, which is becoming more complex. The middle class is becoming stronger and parties are becoming correspondingly weaker.

The old style was a stage, perhaps even a necessary one, in the process of transition in Venezuela. Old-style politics played a useful role and were instrumental in the installation of the democratic system. Now, it may

Diego Abente is associate professor of political science at Miami University of Ohio.

VENEZUELAN POLITICS AND POLICYMAKING

no longer be the answer to Venezuela's problems. Although it certainly represents a fundamental and necessary improvement, I am reluctant to draw too sharp a line or too strong a distinction between the political and the programmatic styles of doing politics. We have different constituencies and conflicts; we have to reconcile the conflicts, and that is politics. There might be changes in the modes and style of politics, in the nature of rewards, but there will be no changes on the issues or in the basic function of politics—the distribution of rewards.

Venezuelans are extremely critical of their own political system. They tend to set unrealistically high standards, resulting in their always being disappointed. The level of participation in the last gubernatorial election was under 50 percent, which was considered a disaster. In the United States we have close to a 50 percent participation rate in presidential elections, and this is supposed to be a successful democracy. With regard to Venezuela, we are talking about a new style of politics and a new style of campaign. Perhaps US politicians can learn something from the Venezuelans.

In many respects, Venezuela is in the vanguard of Latin American nations with regard to the transition to and consolidation of democracy. Many problems remain, of course, but much has been achieved.

13

Discussion

Marcos Mamalakis (University of Wisconsin, Milwaukee): When we try to formulate policies in Latin America, some issues need clarification. One of the most important concerns use of the term "market." We talk about "market" versus "nonmarket" economies, but this is basically a false distinction. The real distinction is between free markets, and distorted or controlled markets. We quite often see the contradiction that arises when we speak in favor of free markets, but then want to control specific prices, for example, the price of oil. This is an internal contradiction. One cannot logically be in favor of a free market and at the same time use this sort of "cafeteria style" approach—which is the typical pattern in Latin America, where everyone wants everyone else's prices to be "free," while his or her own prices have to be controlled.

Neither can a country have a "cafeteria style" political, economic, and social democracy. There are either equal political, economic, and social rights, or there is a potpourri of varying degrees of such rights that negates the very functioning of political, economic, and social systems. The free market is the central issue, whether the parties want completely free markets or not. The minute there is one distortion, the whole system is distorted and tends to disintegrate.

We talk about the withdrawal of the government as a producer of private commodities. But we never talk about the withdrawal of the government from the production of collective commodities, in which literally every Latin American government has been inefficient. To succeed in democracy and economic development, the government has to produce far more and in better quality. So it is not a matter of less government or more government, it is what the nature of government is going to be. The central issue is whether the collective commodities that the state is supposed to produce are produced efficiently through a political party system, so that private commodities can be produced correctly and semipublic commodities, such as administration, health, education, and welfare—which is where the state and the private sector intermingle—can also be produced efficiently.

Unfortunately, we economists have not done a good job. We have never taught the general public in sociology, politics, and so forth what the conceptual framework is; therefore, there is confusion and policies are formulated, whether by one party or another, that are not necessarily coherent and can even be contradictory.

Larry Diamond: There is clearly an attempt being made to change formal political institutions in Venezuela. Minister Blanco wrote about decentralization, administrative reform, electoral reform, and so on. But political institutions cannot be changed in isolation; they are part of a social structure; they are embedded in political culture. Political parties have already been explicitly mentioned. There is going to be an effort to make them more internally democratic and competitive, more programmatic, less clientelistic.

It is healthy that Venezuela plans to adopt a professional, technocratic, and substantive approach to policymaking. But there must be a political coalition behind policies to implement them and maintain them over a period of time long enough to enable them to work. Political parties are important as organizations for the mobilization of support. It may be that, given the changing nature of the economy, it is no longer possible to have consensus in Venezuela. Restructuring involves choices. It is going to create some winners and some losers, and it is an illusion to think that everybody is going to be able to agree on these policies. But it is also an illusion to think that there is no need to mobilize and construct a *political* coalition of enough winners and enough people to see at least the long-run benefits, so they can be viable policies.

There is also a problem that pervades the fate of political parties all over the world: In the age of modern mass communications, particularly television, they become increasingly peripheralized. Television enables presidents and political leaders to go directly to the people and bypass party and political organization. There is an element of danger in this, so political parties should not be allowed to atrophy.

With respect to interest groups, direct subsidies from patrons to particular clients have had great impact. These subsidies are individual benefits that do not really serve the greater public interest. Perhaps the move to modern politics will involve the creation of interest groups for more indirect benefits, rooted in policy rather than in particularistic, rent-seeking payments. There must be a change in political culture, a deep and long-lasting change in public expectations of the state and parties. Such change is imperative because the pressure for clientelism is not just from the top down; it also pushes from the bottom up through the popular expectations of political leaders. This change involves political education to some extent. A change in economic culture is also needed—a change in the way individuals look at their role in society and a realization that there has to be a real linkage between efforts and rewards. Rewards cannot just come through the seeking of favors.

Finally, there has to be a broader kind of normative change that can only be sustained by changes in the legal system, with an independent judiciary as an arbiter of conflicts of interest. If corruption is to be removed from public life or even just better controlled, there must be an aggressive and independent legal system and a strong code of conduct that is independently enforced. Economic opportunities for corruption may have declined along with the reversal of the oil boom and the coming of scarcity and realism, but to the extent that corruption remains in public life, it generates cynicism about politics.

Miriam Kornblith (Central University of Venezuela, Caracas): It was argued that one of Venezuela's greatest advantages was its immense reservoir of political legitimacy and institutional stability. But to what extent have the changes from 1983 to date exhausted this reservoir, and to what extent is this reservoir being refilled? There are worrisome signs in the political system emanating from the leadership, the masses, and from associational life that there has been a serious loss of legitimacy in Venezuela.

There has not been the ability to create new sources of consensus and a legitimate relationship to the system, either in the socioeconomic realm or the political realm. We are witnessing a worsening of the quality of life of the poor and the middle class. From the socioeconomic point of view, there has not been a reestablishment of the links through which the people feel attached to the political system. From the political point of view, as well, the new measures—like the elections of governors and mayors—apparently have not been received with much enthusiasm.

What we are seeing now is the loss of power of the conventional or old sources of consensus and legitimacy and the creation of a vacuum. There is no strong menu of new sources of consensus. We used to think that the state and the parties were the source of all good things and that the private sector was the realm of particularistic interest. Today, the good guys are the private sector and the bad guys are the parties and state. Our approach should be more balanced.

Perhaps we are witnessing a shift from a populist paternalism to a liberal or technocratic paternalism. Basically we may still be approaching the relationship between leader and civil society from a paternalistic point of view, but now in a more liberal sense, although it is still patronizing in many ways.

Gilbert Richardson (American Association for the Study of the United States in World Affairs): One of the favorite harassments of Western Europeans is to catch a covey of US citizens in Europe and ask them what form of government they have, a democracy or a republic. About one-third will

141

usually say that we have a democracy, another third that we have a republic, and the remaining third say that they do not know.

Our founding fathers made a strong distinction between a democracy and a republic. James Madison said that a democracy is a small piece of government where everyone speaks for themselves, such as in a New England town hall. But Article 4, Section 4, of the Constitution of the United States prescribes a republican form of government, that is, one in which someone else is elected to speak for you. The Supreme Court says that if it is not in the Constitution it is not our form of government, but the word "democracy" does not appear in the Constitution. Thus, we might have to say that a democracy is an unconstitutional form of government.

We pour democracy on everything as if it were ketchup and we set bad examples for our young students if we do not tell them that our priority is a republican form of government, one in which somebody else speaks for us. Our "Pledge of Allegiance" is "to the flag of the United States of America and to the republic for which it stands."

Moisés Naím: A point made earlier concerning what seems to be a strong contradiction is well taken. What does it mean to privatize companies if we have a private sector that does not work? It would be unwise to transfer to an inefficient private sector inefficient companies now in the hands of government. Reference was made to the Venezuelan Development Corporation (CVF), which was a good idea that was not well implemented. It was a government-owned institution to promote industrial expansion, to make soft loans for new industrial ventures and initiatives. In some cases it gave guarantees that should a company fail, the CVF would be in charge of repaying the debt. The CVF could also hold a minority share in a company.

Over the years, that became a nightmare, and all of those guarantees became a debt of the republic. It had become a sophisticated ploy to export capital goods to Venezuela. An exporter could establish a company in Venezuela to buy machines to be exported. Or the machines did not work or no one bought the products that were made by the company. The company went bankrupt, and the state had to pay the credits with which the machines were bought.

It is not correct to draw a parallel between that process and the desire to sell some of our state-owned enterprises that cost Venezuela billions of bolivars each year. If the government does not operate a shipping or airline company, someone in the private sector can, probably even better. But if we do not build sewers and if we do not develop social programs, no one else is going to do that for the government.

A second point is that the private sector is neither inherently efficient nor inefficient. The companies in our private sector are just a reflection of the environment that was created for them. Why should they be efficient if they are operating under conditions in which they are over-protected, in which they do not have to worry about costs, competition, or efficiency? Why should they be efficient if they can make more money with the signature of a bureaucrat than with systematic efforts to increase productivity?

What we did for many years in Venezuela was to create incentives for the private sector to invest in good lawyers and public relations people to develop good relationships with government ministries. But we did not create the incentives to hire the best engineers, productivity experts, and marketing people. What we are talking about now is a new atmosphere, a different framework to generate other kinds of investment opportunities and other kinds of incentives. There is no need now for a company to invest in inviting me to dinner. It is more to their advantage to try to develop new export markets and find new joint ventures.

We also assumed that the nationality of the shareholders would be the major determinant in the behavior of a private firm, that foreign firms would behave differently from local firms and pursue strategies that might run against the interests of the country. Thus, in order to protect local firms, we created a restrictive environment for foreign investment. But the decade in which we had the most control over foreign investment and foreign exchange was the decade we received the most foreign capital. We have no evidence to support the notion that Venezuelan-owned companies behaved any more nationalistically than foreign companies. The main assumption on which we are basing our current economic policies is that a private company is a private company, and its behavior is not controlled by the nationalities of its shareholders but by the favorable climate that is created for it.

Thus, when we talk about privatization we do not mean, for instance, selling the shipping line to some merchant marine officer who only knows how to run a heavily subsidized and protected shipping line. It means turning to some of the great merchant marine companies of the world that can run an efficient system. We do not want a private sector of only Venezuelan firms, but a private sector of the world.

Andrés Stambouli: The new policymaking style is, as a matter of fact, a more isolated style in Venezuelan democracy, but it does not represent authoritarianism. There is a problem about the notion of constituency, accountability, and representation. Constituency is not the same in Venezuela as it is in the United States because in Venezuela political parties and political leaders do not have issue-oriented constituencies. They have priority-oriented constituencies—not even constituencies, but radicalism and partisanship. What we want to do with the state reform movement is to have real constituencies, to have a public that is able to debate the issues, not just a general leadership to whom we give carte blanche.

The first government of Carlos Andrés Pérez was nonpartisan. But the opposition inside his party was opposed to the leadership, asking, Why is he there and not I? President Pérez reached a consensus with the opposition. It was not a consensus based on debate and negotiation, but on how much and what to receive in exchange for participation. And that is why, in recent years, the system became explosive.

I do not mean to give the impression that old-style politics were "bad" and new-style politics are "good." Rather, the old style is exhausted and we must renovate the old forms to pursue new goals.

We should not set voter turnout as a standard by which to measure the success of democracy. In any society that can provide for its basic needs, and where there is no threat to the legitimacy of the political system, low voter turnout does not necessarily reflect a rejection of the central values of democracy. But when you have 50 and 60 percent abstention in a society like Venezuela or Colombia, it means that the population is rejecting the politicians and their politics. I fully agree with Larry Diamond that technocrats should be wary of saying that politics is no longer necessary. There is a dangerous erosion of legitimacy in Venezuela. We need a new kind of consensus now, one not based on abundance but oriented toward a new public philosophy, a new national project.

We must seek the delicate equilibrium between policymaking and decisionmaking without general consensus. We must avoid authoritarianism or authoritarian democracy. And we must avoid the point at which democracy breaks down as a result of an insistence on decisionmaking without general consensus. A consensus-style democracy for Venezuela is not sustainable if we do not start to construct constituencies. Today we are on the road toward pluralistic democracy, which means accountability, constituencies, and an issue-oriented society.

PART 5

EPILOGUE

14

The Political Management of Radical Economic Change: Lessons from the Venezuelan Experience

Moisés Naím

The evening of that first Sunday of February was somewhat tense at the convention center in the small alpine town of Davos in Switzerland. The tension was not only because the most important plenary session of the 1992 annual gathering of the more than one thousand leading business-people, politicians, academics, and government officials from all over the world was taking place. The issues being addressed also created a certain amount of uneasiness among the attendees. That evening, two panel discussions were being held, dealing with highly charged and problem-atic regional situations bearing substantial repercussions for the rest of the world. The first was about the transition in South Africa, with Nelson Mandela, Chief Buthelezi, and President De Klerk as panelists. The second had Henry Kissinger moderating a panel of seven former com-munist bosses who were now the democratically elected presidents of independent republics in the former Soviet Union.

In order, perhaps, to provide a contrast in regional perspective and offer a respite from the gloomy conclusions that, in all probability, were going to be drawn from these two panels, the organizers had sandwiched in between the two, the presentation of Venezuelan president Carlos Andrés Pérez. As expected, Pérez offered all sorts of good news in his speech, showing that painful transitions toward free markets pay off, and that a democratic regime can indeed survive the unpopular decisions required by economic reforms.

He could back such important claims with hard facts. In 1991, not only had inflation and unemployment declined for a second consecutive year, but the country's economy experienced the highest growth rate in the world, and the highest in the country's history. Institutional reforms of all kinds were gaining speed and the privatization process was an internationally recognized model of effectiveness and clarity. Only two years after having been cut off from the international credit markets, Venezuela was now enjoying the renewed confidence of both lenders and investors. In fact, international credit rating agencies had just upgraded

Moisés Naím is senior associate of the Carnegie Endowment for International Relations.

the country's rating, and other publications specializing in assessing investment climates were ranking Venezuela at the top of their world lists, together with Mexico and Chile, as the preferred investment location in the region.[1]

The following evening was even more tense for Carlos Andrés Pérez. He was bombed out of his office at the presidential palace after having fled his residence, minutes before a group of rebel paratroopers started lobbing mortar shells inside the compound.

President Pérez survived the attempt on his life and regained control of the situation a few hours after the attempted coup, thus also preserving democracy for Venezuela. But from that day on, he had to preside over a very different country. The failed coup unleashed a political process that is bound to have significant, irreversible and, to a large extent, unpredictable consequences for the country's future.

What happened? How could it happen? What does it mean? Does it mean, perhaps, that if one of the developing world's oldest democracies cannot withstand the political consequences of market reforms, others, not as blessed by democratic longevity and oil, should conclude that the transition to a market economy is incompatible with a liberal democracy? Should proponents of gradualism in economic reform rest their case on the evidence provided by the Venezuelan experience? If a country gets this kind of political instability after two consecutive years of high growth, what should other countries expect, for which adjustment means many years of recession, inflation, and growing unemployment? What lessons can be drawn from the failed coup in Venezuela?

The purpose of the following pages is to sketch some highly preliminary answers to these questions.

The Coup

The day after his speech in Davos, the president took a commercial flight back to Venezuela, arriving at the airport the evening of Monday, February 3. To his surprise, he found the defense minister waiting for him at the gate and then he noticed an unprecedented display of soldiers at the airport. The minister informed him that he took military control of the airport as a precaution against an attack by rebel units within the army. He had been notified by the army's counterintelligence directorate of an impending attack by army units against the president upon his return from Switzerland (*El Nacional,* March 9, 1992).

From the airport, the president's motorcade went to the official residence of La Casona. After a brief stop there, he went to his office at Miraflores, the presidential palace located at the opposite end of Caracas. Between midnight and 1 A.M. on February 4, a group of soldiers, heavily armed and backed by armored vehicles, started to attack Miraflores. Other rebel units attacked La Casona and the nearby Francisco de Miranda air base, where the air force headquarters are located. Rebel troops also tried and failed to take over the headquarters of the government intelligence services (DISIP) but were successful in surrounding and blocking traffic to and from the army and navy headquarters and the Ministry of Defense.

President Pérez barely escaped being killed or captured by the rebels by exiting the palace through a back door, hiding under a coat in the back seat of an unmarked car. He went to a private television station from which he contacted loyal army chiefs and managed to broadcast a speech to the nation. In it, he explained that an attempt against his life had taken place, that with the exception of the small group of individuals participating in the uprising, the rest of the armed forces were loyal to the Constitution and, therefore, to him as the democratically elected president and commander in chief of the armed forces. He emphasized that the coup could not succeed, that loyal forces were in the process of regaining control of the situation, and that he had already received personal calls from President Bush, from most Latin American presidents, and other world leaders to express their solidarity and full support for his government.[2]

The president was soon joined at the television station by Eduardo Fernández, the secretary-general of COPEI, the main opposition party, who around 2:30 A.M. also went on the air to give an impassioned speech stating that he, too, was opposed to the government, but that the only acceptable way to express such disagreement was through votes, not bullets. A while later, the president spoke again to inform the nation that most rebel forces had surrendered and exhorted those few still fighting to cease fire and give up their resistance. The heads of the main political parties, the CTV (the workers' federation) and of FEDECAMARAS (the private sector federation) also appeared on television to condemn the uprising and express their organizations' support for democracy and constitutional rule.

At about 5 A.M., President Pérez went back on the air, this time from Miraflores Palace, together with the ministers of defense and the interior, to state that his government had complete control of the situation and that all the leaders of the revolt were under arrest.

Just as he had done during the February 1989 riots, Pérez was compelled at midmorning to convene his cabinet and pass a decree suspending constitutional guarantees. At the same time that he was in his cabinet meeting reviewing the situation with his ministers, he had to respond to several phone calls from the military command requesting his authorization to allow the arrested leader of the coup—38-year-old Lieutenant-Colonel Hugo Chávez, to go on television to ask the rebels who were still resisting in different parts of the country to surrender, in order to avoid further bloodshed. The president had already refused, on several occasions since the beginning of the revolt, to negotiate with the rebels, even having at one point to vehemently order the defense minister: "I do not want negotiations of any kind, General, give them bullets!" Just before noon, he finally approved the request to broadcast a videotaped and *edited* message from Lieutenant Colonel Chávez. Instead, Chávez appeared *live*, for under two minutes, on a nationally broadcast message that contributed more to destabilizing the Venezuelan democracy than all the shots fired through the night.[3] Impeccably dressed in his uniform, and without showing any signs of fatigue or stress, he eloquently delivered a short speech emphasizing his Bolivarian values, and stressing that among other things, "unfortunately, *for now*, the objectives we sought were not achieved in the capital city. That is, we in Caracas could not gain control of power. You, there in the interior, did a great job. But it is time now to avoid further bloodshed; it is time to reflect. We will have new situations. The country definitely has to embark on the road to a better destiny." (*El Universal,* February 5, 1992, as reprinted by Ponce [1992:11]; M. Naím translation.)

In his televised address, Chávez accepted full responsibility for the uprising and said that he was prepared to bear the consequences of his actions. A public figure acknowledging that he personally failed while others did "a great job," who maintains an unfaltering position even after failure and defeat, who faces his responsibility and does not try to evade the repercussions of his actions, was an uncommon sight for television viewers accustomed to watching the verbal and political maneuverings of traditional politicians. But, more than anything else, this televised image conveyed the possibility of change, of immediate discontinuity with political and economic schemes usually blamed for the country's problems. A new face, unrelated to the power structures that had traditionally dominated political and economic life in the country, offering to guide the nation back to the promised land of prosperity, equality, and honesty, was a product that, regardless of its packaging, was bound to be very appealing to a mass audience. The fact that the packaging was a primitive army tyrant was easy to bury under the illusion that change, any change, meant progress.

But Chávez's televised address was not the only one that created the conditions for the political backlash that Pérez and his government had to endure after surviving the coup. Rafael Caldera, a respected former president (1968 to 1973) and founder of the Christian Democratic party (COPEI) also took advantage of the situation to promote his views. On the afternoon of February 4, Congress met in an emergency session to consider and eventually approve the government's request to endorse the cabinet decree temporarily suspending constitutional guarantees. A speedy agreement had been reached by all major political parties to support the lifting of the guarantees, and no speeches were scheduled. But to everyone's surprise, former president Caldera, one of the founding fathers of democracy in Venezuela, requested and was granted the right to speak at the session that was being broadcast by the official TV and radio stations and retransmitted by all others. Caldera then proceeded to deliver a message that left congressmen shocked, the government bewildered, and his popularity ratings among the population many percentage points higher than they had been before the address. In it, he briefly condemned the idea of taking power by force, but then devoted most of his time to explain that the motives of the rebels were amply justified by the country's situation. Among other things, he insisted that the economic policies being pursued had left Venezuelans so poor and in such miserable conditions that no one had the right to ask the people to sacrifice in the name of democracy. He concluded by asking President Pérez to correct his mistakes and "rectify" his economic program.[4]

From then on, the political situation started to deteriorate very rapidly for Pérez and his government. As one observer noted, the coup was retroactively "kidnapped" by Chávez and Caldera with the great help of the government's own TV cameras. In fact, the historical significance of the attempted coup will probably lie more in the profound changes it induced in Venezuelan democratic politics and democratic institutions than in its effect on the political role of the military or on civil-military relations in the country.

Paradoxically, and in contrast with the February 1989 riots, when several weeks had to pass before normalcy gradually emerged, the events of February 1992 did not generate major interruptions of the day-to-day routines of Venezuelans. In fact, the day after the coup and the televised speeches, economic life proceeded as usual, with shops, businesses, schools, and government offices opening and functioning as if nothing had happened. The same was not true for the political system.

The After-Coup: A Political Hangover

While the coup failed to overthrow the government, it was very successful in unleashing the deepest political crisis the country had faced since democracy was restored in 1958. After the attempted coup several facts about its leaders became apparent, at the same time that different political trends emerged with great force.

The leaders of the failed coup were four lieutenant colonels[5] who were well known amongst their colleagues for their critical views of the democratic regime and for the bluntness and relative openness with which, for many years, they had been privately espousing the need for the armed forces to play a much greater role in running the country. Their ideological discourse centered almost exclusively on repeated references to the ideas and writings of Simón Bolívar, the insistence that the corruption of the ruling classes had to be stopped by any means, and that the armed forces should not allow the politicians in government to bargain away Venezuela's rights to Colombia in the century-old border dispute between the two countries.[6] Although these officers had some systematic contacts with the radical left, no major linkages or alliances with other organized civil or military groups was evident. In fact, the four officers belonged to the same graduating class from the military academy and seemed to maintain a close-knit and rather isolated group within the military.

The coup's failure was to a great extent due to President Pérez's instincts and quick reactions, but also to the lack of initial support for the rebels on the part of the military and of the people at the time of the uprising, to major blunders in the planning and execution of their actions, and to mere chance.[7] Although they were able to enter the capital, attack, and eventually control major strategic objectives and also control certain significant sites in the cities of Maracaibo, Maracay, and Valencia, preliminary estimates indicate that only a very small fraction of the armed forces took active part in the revolt.[8]

The attempted coup's near-success can be attributed to major errors and omissions within the armed forces and other government security agencies. As noted, the leaders of the uprising were well known, and rumors about their intentions had been circulating for years within the armed forces. Their planning meetings were held with a minimum of disguise and caution, and the day before the uprising, information about it was known and largely ignored by higher echelons within the army (*El Nacional*, March 9, 1992). The rebels were able to enter Caracas through a main highway in broad daylight by bus, heavily armed and undisguised, without activating any of the warning mechanisms that any state or army normally has. Much can be made of these facts as evidence of generalized military complicity with the plotters. Nonetheless, an alternative and perhaps more plausible explanation would stress the complacency bred by many years of democracy, plus the institutional decay that characterized all the different organs of the Venezuelan state, which seriously undermined its capacity to react effectively and efficiently. Furthermore, the fact that the media had been echoing and amplifying mostly baseless rumors about an "imminent" coup since the beginning of the Pérez administration is bound to have eroded the alertness of the units in charge of intelligence and state security. In sum, the fact that the armed forces are part and parcel of a greatly weakened and institutionally devastated state in which authority and efficiency are rare phenomena should be taken into consideration in any assessment of the behavior of the armed forces in this event.

Explanations about the coup that stress its economic, social, and political determinants are valid, and these are discussed below. However, it is important to keep in mind that the coup would have never occurred—or would have had a much smaller impact—if it were not for the fact that the state had lost the capacity to perform even the most rudimentary security services needed to ensure its own survival. After all, these events were staged by four rather isolated individuals able to persuade or coerce a relatively small number of their subordinates, while the state was capable of reacting effectively only after the main sites of power were being bombed.

The uprising, together with Caldera's and Chávez's speeches, galvanized the opposition against Pérez and his government. Their actions blew the lid off any inhibition to protest. (See the appendixes at chapter's end.) Thus, passive social groups and respected individuals became active and very vocal in expressing their dissatisfaction with a government that not only pursued highly unpopular policies, but was also blamed for having jeopardized the country's democratic stability. Furthermore, the fact that immediately after the events the possibility of another coup by the military was not completely dispelled, that Pérez looked weak, and that his party (Acción Democrática) did not act decisively to support him during the night of the coup, precipitated a major wave of political attacks against the president that culminated with generalized calls for his resignation. Although labor unions, the private sector, the public bureaucracy, all political parties, professional associations, university professors and students, farmers, the armed forces, media owners, the middle class and, in general, almost all sectors and groups of society had seen some of their privileges taken away and each had its specific grudge against the government, their convergence had never been possible until the coup.

Some, especially certain traditional factions within the political parties, emphasized the need for a radical reversal of economic policy. Others insisted that the country's crisis was essentially political and ethical, and that the concentration of power in the traditional political parties had bred the widespread corruption that was eroding all of society. A lot of finger pointing took place, but at the end of the day, most fingers pointed at President Pérez, either blaming him for his painful economic policies or for having been too indecisive in the fight against corruption.

It became obvious that in order to survive the government needed to broaden its base of support and promote a number of political and institutional reforms. Pérez embarked on intense consultations with a wide variety of groups and individuals, while acting on different fronts. The political dynamics of the country acquired a dazzling speed, and institutional instability reached unprecedented levels. Witness, for example, some of the changes that the government either implemented or tried to implement in a six-week period following the failed coup:

- A major reshuffling of the command structure of the armed forces, whereby the president, together with the minister of defense and the joint chiefs of staff, replaced some of the senior officers holding operational command posts at the time of the attempted coup.

- The government's decision to utilize the temporary suspension of constitutional guarantees to curb the inflammatory excesses of the media by sending government officials to censor the information before it was printed or broadcast. Not surprisingly, the decision backfired, leaving the government in the worst of both worlds. It had to bear the enormous political cost that such a decision invariably carries, even as it discovered that it lacked the capacity to ensure that censorship was effectively implemented. A short time after it was enacted and after being universally condemned at home and abroad, the government had to reverse its decision.

- A cabinet change in which the president attempted, and largely failed, to incorporate prestigious individuals or members of other political parties, whose presence in the government would broaden its support base. The president removed the president of the Central Bank, appointing to that post the minister of planning, Miguel Rodríguez, the main architect of the economic reform program. However, only a few weeks later, Rodríguez had to step down in the face of strong political protests over his appointment. The minister of the Interior and a few other cabinet members of lesser political significance were also replaced. Having failed to convince most of the individuals to whom he offered major cabinet posts to join, President Pérez appointed them to a newly created advisory council.

- The relative failure to form a more broadly based cabinet was another confirmation of Pérez's political weakness at that time and thus was a great spur to his opponents. Calls for the president's resignation intensified, as well as demands for the dismissal of Congress and its temporary substitution by an elected group charged with reforming the Constitution. There were also strong demands for the restructuring of the Supreme Court of Justice and the replacement of its current members—most of them political appointees representing either Acción Democrática or COPEI—with independent judges, as well as a major reform of the highly corrupt and inefficient judicial system. The political environment became even more charged and tense.

- In a long-awaited speech about two weeks after the modification of the cabinet, the president announced major changes, new social measures, fundamental proposals for legislative action, and some corrections to his economic program. These announcements somewhat helped to reduce the political agitation.[9]

- A few days after this speech, the president again reshuffled his cabinet, removing nine ministers. He was able to incorporate several new individuals who were either members of COPEI or closely affiliated with that party. That agreement between the government and COPEI in turn lasted only a few weeks, after which COPEI decided that it would no longer be willing to be associated with the Pérez administration and asked its members holding cabinet posts to resign.[10]

In the subsequent months, calls for Pérez's resignation continued. It became evident, however, that Pérez was not going to resign and that calls for him to do so came from individuals and groups who were unable to do anything more than voice such demands through the media. Although street demonstrations and protests became relatively more frequent, they were mostly concentrated among small radical student groups that took advantage of the government's inability to contain their street actions effectively.

The government continued to seek some form of alliance with other political forces, without much success. Different groups of businessmen, civic leaders, and other organizations attempted, also without success, to create a platform for different types of a broad-based "National Alliance."

Pérez patiently waited for the political turbulence to die down. With presidential elections scheduled for December 1993, the main political actors in a state of internal disarray, and without strong leadership or a coherent political strategy, the incentives to lie low and just wait for his term to end became obvious. Although strong criticisms against the president and the government continued unabated, no individual or political group had sufficient power to go any further except to veto the initiatives of others. Although this stalemate made it very difficult for the Pérez administration to maintain the rapid pace its reform program had attained in its first three years, it also made it equally impossible for groups opposing the reforms to impose reversals of any major significance.

This is not to say, of course, that the instability did not take its toll. The international enthusiasm about investing in Venezuela which had reached an all-time high just before the coup, decreased sharply; difficulties generating Congressional support to pass tax laws, desperately needed to avoid a sharp deterioration of the fiscal stance, became enormous; and the turnover among government technocrats even further weakened the technical capacity of the government to design and execute public policies.

The long-term consequences of the coup and its aftermath are difficult to appraise. But an understanding of the nature of the circumstances that brought them about can certainly provide interesting insights into the political challenges of managing large-scale economic change.

The Determinants of the Coup: The Military and the Erosion of the Power of the Pyramid

The attempted coup and the turbulent political and social situation it catalyzed were, of course, the product of several forces acting simultaneously. The situation within the armed forces was a natural expression of the general situation of the country, the state of the economy, and the widespread dissatisfaction with living standards. The universal frustration with an incompetent and corrupt state also added to a complex situation characterized by instability and uncertainty. It was this highly unstable setting that led the plotters to believe that a coup was possible and that it would be widely supported. With time, a more complete and historically grounded perspective about the failed coup will certainly emerge. It is, nonetheless, still possible at this point to identify some of the factors that will have to be taken into account in any future examination of this process.

Several long-standing trends had been shaping the functioning and internal culture of the Venezuelan armed forces. The first is that, for many years, the promotion system was gradually relaxed. This relaxation allowed the number of senior officers to increase at a much faster pace than the number of positions available. This trend, which greatly accelerated in the eighties, systematically eroded the hierarchical pyramid on which much of military organization and life is based. In effect, each year it became easier to find generals tending posts that only a few years before were assigned to captains.

The fact that too many generals and admirals were chasing too few "real" jobs within the armed forces made merit a necessary but not sufficient condition for promotion and career advancement. This in turn spurred a very strong rivalry between individuals and the small informal groups or "clans" to which they belonged. Therefore, significant incentives existed for aspiring officers and their mentors and protégées to direct some efforts to block or even sabotage the career development and the possibilities for promotion of their rivals.[11]

The weight of factors not directly related to the individual's merit in promotion decisions is further intensified by the fact that by law, after a certain rank, promotions have to be authorized by Congress. In this way, a mechanism originally envisioned as a healthy check by civil society over the military became a factor of politization, scarcely muted partisanship, and a boost for the exclusionary tactics in which rival officers and their clans commonly engaged.

All this implies that the interservice rivalries that shape the organizational behavior of the military everywhere acquire—under these circumstances—an even more important role. Competition for budgets, resources, and career opportunities develops not only among the army, the navy, and the air force, but is intensely replicated and multiplied within each branch, as well. The competition was rendered even more intense by the fiscal crisis of the eighties, when military budgets were tightened and the foreign exchange required for arms procurement and maintenance became more expensive each year and, therefore, less available.

Another consequence of the fiscal crisis was that while an increasing portion of the military budget was allocated to foreign exchange, the daily needs of soldiers and junior officers were left grossly underfunded. At the same time that major outlays were made for the purchase of F-16 fighter planes, sophisticated French tanks, and Italian warships, soldiers had to live with an inadequate supply of boots, uniforms, housing, and implements to cover their basic needs. Salaries of junior officers eroded to such a degree that they could no longer afford a car or even adequate housing. In fact, it became common for junior officers to pool their families together and share a single apartment in poor barrios. This created strong resentment toward senior officers, who became increasingly isolated from their subordinates and preoccupied with the economics of procurement and the politics of promotion. The lack of cohesion between junior officers and their superiors was also exacerbated by the fact that while the current generation of junior officers had ample opportunities to complement its military education with professional studies at home and abroad, that was not the case with older officers. These were part of the cohort of officers whose academic training in the mid-1960s had been cut short by the need to respond to the demands on personnel created at the time by the war against the leftist guerillas. All this contributed greatly to the tensions and climate of mistrust between senior officers and their subordinates, thus adding to the erosion of discipline and to organizational decay and fragmentation.

Finally, two traits common to all public sector organizations in Venezuela also greatly affected the armed forces: turnover and lack of clear and stable organizational goals. The average tenure of the minister of Defense—who has always been a senior military officer—is one year. After that year in the cabinet, he normally reaches retirement age and has to step down both from government and from active duty in the military. Needless to say, such a turnover is another source of instability, politicking, and inefficiency within the armed forces, greatly hampering any sustained effort aimed at institutional building and organizational development. The second source of instability is the rapidly changing domestic and international conditions that have created a great deal of confusion regarding the precise role of the armed forces in a country with the geopolitical, social, and economic characteristics of Venezuela. This, in turn, has also contributed to the blurring of a unified and shared vision essential to maintaining a common sense of direction within a complex organization.

The end result of all these forces operating within the armed forces should come as no surprise: centralized authority and control are difficult to maintain, and the institutional problems of the military reflect those of most other social institutions. These factors should be carefully assessed in any evaluation of the attempted coup.

The Economy: The Insufficiency of World Records

In 1991, Venezuela had the world's fastest growing economy. With 9.2 percent GNP growth, it surpassed economic powerhouses like Singapore (6.5 percent), Malaysia (8.6 percent), Thailand (7.9 percent), and Indonesia (7 percent). Venezuela's expansion of output in 1991 went far beyond that experienced on average by the major industrial countries (2 percent) and by Latin America as a whole (2.6 percent).[12]

It was a year in which 431,000 new jobs were created in the private sector—the largest increase in more than a decade—thus boosting the size of the formally employed population in that sector to an unprecedented 4.2 million workers. Additionally, the size of the informal sector diminished for the first time in eight years (by 129,000 persons), and total unemployment decreased by 85,000 citizens, thus reducing the unemployment rate from almost 10 percent the previous year to 8.5 percent.

Also in 1991, the current account of the balance of payments showed a surplus of about US $8 billion; international reserves reached US $14 billion, while the stock of foreign investment advanced to its highest level since the mid-1970s. The fiscal deficit was less than 3 percent, the exchange rate remained extremely stable, and the stock market had a second boom year with a rise of 64 percent (or 35.2 percent if measured in US dollars).[13]

But 1991 was a good year not only in terms of macroeconomic aggregates. It was a year in which the unit volume of domestic consumption in poultry increased by 41 percent, rice increased by 30 percent, pasta (a major food staple among low income groups) by 25 percent, sugar by 20 percent, and it was also a year in which the food processing industry in general expanded by 11 percent in volume. Furthermore, in 1991 the apparel market grew by 28 percent (excluding imports), the number of cars sold increased 72 percent over the previous year, and the household appliance sector had its strongest season ever.[14]

All these record-setting numbers created great enthusiasm among businessmen, government officials, and foreign investors, but not among local politicians, journalists, and other opinionmakers who, by and large, remained unfazed by the statistics and highly critical of the government's economic policies. In many cases, these criticisms were motivated by the particular interests of the widowers of the previous system—individuals and groups that lost privileges and power under the new scheme and longed for a return to the former, more comfortable and more profitable ways. But there were other, more disinterested observers who also expressed great concern about the situation, not to mention, of course, the general dissatisfaction among the population with the country's situation.

An inflationary level (31 percent in 1991 and 36.5 percent in 1990) that continued to erode the buying power of the poor and the middle classes remained a major source of social friction. While in 1991 real salaries increased for the first time after many years, they were still lagging behind the needs and expectations created by decades of an artificial economy that had become unaffordable. Unhappiness with inflation was further amplified by the fact that the government's efforts to target special social programs directly to the poor were also lagging far behind needs and expectations.[15] Massive and largely inefficient subsidies can be eliminated almost instantaneously. Building the institutions required to deliver the assistance to highly vulnerable target groups takes much longer. As is being discovered by all countries undergoing major structural reforms, social safety nets are much easier to design than to implement. Furthermore, the capacity of the state to supply basic services in health, housing, education, or urban transportation had also been drastically reduced by a decade of fiscal crises and mismanagement, a situation aggravated by the economic adjustment process, and the ineffectiveness and delays of government actions on this front. Inefficient and insufficient public services were a cause of continuous anger against the government and of dismissal of its claims of macroeconomic success.

The effects on public opinion of hospitals that do not work, an unreliable and insufficient water supply system, a public bus system that never runs on time and never has service adequate to move urban workers to and from their jobs, and a school system in shambles, obviously all have devastating consequences for government popularity. The negative attitudes toward a government brought about by such concrete public problems cannot be expected to be offset by news of a solid balance of payments, or a world record in terms of GNP growth.

Furthermore, it was perceived that no explicit effort was being made towards the rectification of the profoundly inequitable income distribution and wealth that many years of demagogic and ill-conceived government intervention had produced. The stock market was soaring, imports of previously banned luxury products filled the shopping malls, and the privileged few that had dollar-denominated savings could flaunt their wealth with a newfound market-ethos. At the same time, however, the great majority of the population saw their paychecks buying much less than what they had been accustomed to for decades.

The government kept insisting that the hardships imposed by the new economic policies were unavoidable. It also insisted that the social costs of its reforms were much lower than those caused by not implementing the corrections and living with the ravaging consequences of hyperinflation. Although this is certainly true, it is also a counterfactual argument that referred to a hypothetical possibility to which most Venezuelans could not relate, either intellectually or experientially. The country had never before experienced anything similar to the situation it was now going through, nor had it ever suffered the ordeals of hyperinflation. Meanwhile, the day-to-day hardships and frustrations were neither remote nor hypothetical. They were perceived as the direct consequences of actions taken by the government.

The economic malaise—attributed by public opinion to politicians in general and to the Pérez government in particular—contributed to the creation of a social and political environment that exacerbated the instability prompted by the aborted coup. Nevertheless, it would be a grievous mistake to conclude that the state of the economy was the fundamental force underlying the Venezuelan political and institutional crisis. The point is that while the economy was rapidly recovering and serious macroeconomic imbalances had been corrected, much more was expected from an economic program that had to substitute for the all-encompassing state-centered approach that had prevailed for many decades. In practice, the economic stabilization program had to fulfill political and ideological functions for which it was not designed and was ill suited (see Chapter 4 in this volume). Furthermore, the new economic policies were generally perceived as the main cause of the operational collapse of public services and social delivery agencies that, for all practical purposes, had been neglected for years and utilized to serve the particular interests of the labor leaders who controlled them and the politicians who appointed the labor leaders. In fact, it could be argued that while the economic crisis was far from over, the economy was rapidly becoming a source of political stability, as small but influential social groups gradually started to support the new market-oriented approach and results were becoming more apparent. But while the economy tended to stabilize, the social and political systems exhibited a disarray that was a powerful source of instability and turmoil.

Politics: Corruption, Oligopolistic Wars, and the Media as Sources of Instability

As mentioned, since the beginning in 1989, the policies of the Pérez government were opposed for various reasons by almost all organized groups of society. Such opposition notwithstanding, the government was able to proceed for three years with the reform program it had designed without having to make any major concessions to those who resisted the changes and fought for the maintenance of the previous scheme. The main reasons for this were that even if the government was politically and institutionally weak, the opposing groups were even weaker and ill prepared to counter the government's initiatives.[16] The government capitalized on such weaknesses and, acting with great speed, was able to implement fundamental macroeconomic reforms, and was even able to move ahead in terms of institutional changes and privatization. But the aborted coup and its political backlash gave to the groups and individuals opposing the reforms the possibility of overcoming their previously demonstrated inability to block the process effectively. After the coup failed, the initial reaction of most politicians was to place all the blame on the economic policies and to stress the need to reverse the changes. But the coup also mobilized other individuals and groups that had not been very active in the political debate, and soon thereafter, traditional politicians were put on the defensive. In fact, criticisms against the behavior and role of political parties, against corruption and the administration of justice, took a strong hold over public opinion and over the general mood of the country. But the magnitude of the political and institutional crisis was not only determined by the interplay between a government wanting to introduce unpopular changes and political groups opposing the changes and jockeying for power. The period of great instability in which the country entered after the revolt was determined by forces deeply ingrained in the moral, social, and political structure of the country as well.

The Role of Corruption

Government corruption is closely related to the extent of the state's intervention in the economy. The more it intervenes, the higher the opportunities for profitable collusion between government officials and those who can benefit from biasing public decisions. Transactions in which the government is either the seller (for example, in all privatizations) or the buyer (for example, in all procurement activities) lead inevitably to bribes and kickbacks when money is exchanged for highways, guns, or food for public hospitals. This is true in all countries. The interesting point to make is that, in contrast to the dominant perception among Venezuelans, there are strong reasons to presume that corruption greatly diminished during the Pérez government. The main reason underlying this presumption is that by eliminating most government controls (on prices, the exchange rate, interest rates, imports and exports, credits, and so forth) the possibilities for government officials to weight a decision in favor of a specific individual or firm were greatly diminished. Furthermore, all the major decisions related to the privatization process (even the hiring of consultants and financial advisors) were arrived at through very open international auctions accessible to all interested parties. Also, given the experience of all countries, where government procurement is a corruption-prone activity, the vigorous and unprecedented media scrutiny over public decisions of the Pérez government is bound to have had at least some degree of influence in curbing excesses that in the past went largely unreported by the mass media and were much more dependent on the government's goodwill for their profitability.

Why then was corruption such a generalized source of dissatisfaction and opposition to the government? There are at least three reasons for this paradox: (1) The bulk of the population had two deeply ingrained beliefs: that Venezuela was a very rich country, and that it was impoverished by the corruption and thievery of the rich and powerful. Instead of blaming macroeconomic mismanagement, external shocks, or incompetence, people blamed the country's economic crisis on corruption. Moreover, the unprecedented daily economic tribulations gave a very concrete and personal meaning to a concept hitherto perceived as just a rather abstract ethical problem of those with political or economic power; (2) Although the government stridently denounced the corruption that accompanied the economic schemes it was dismantling, it was very ineffective in bringing to justice those suspected of having been involved in corrupt practices. In fact, the government was widely perceived as being soft to the point of complicity in the punishment of individuals who took open advantage of the existing opportunities for corruption; and (3) The media echoed and heightened the frustration of the population and was more active and audacious than ever in denouncing corruption, and bringing it to the forefront of public discussions of any and all matters of government and public policy. This stood in sharp contrast to the fact that in almost all prosecuted cases, the accused were found innocent by the courts or were able to flee the country. Corruption and its economic and political consequences created the classic case where anger and hunger combined to create a very explosive political and social ferment.

The most important point to understand is that one of the side effects of the economic reforms was that the tolerance and passivity Venezuelans had tended to exhibit toward corruption greatly diminished. Unfortunately, this unexpected new demand for justice and the punishment of those involved in corruption scandals could not be effectively satisfied by a judicial system that had never before been subjected to such demands, and which was itself paralyzed by corruption and incompetence.

The Unanticipated Political Consequences of Breaking Down Oligopolies

The fact that entrenched oligopolies will fight against any attempt to change public policies restricting competition should come as no surprise. In fact, this was yet another source of opposition to the Pérez government. But what turned out to be a much stronger source of political instability was the oligopolistic wars that broke out among different conglomerates or economic groups as a result of the competition induced by deregulation. This was an economic phenomenon of profound and largely unexpected political consequences.

Many years of intense government intervention create market structures wherein competition is dormant and oligopolistic behavior prevalent. Under such conditions, private firms have incentives to court government officials and politicians whose decisions can make or break a business. Trying to check the advances of the few rivals with whom they have to share the market and compete for scarce resources and inputs is also a dominant objective of firms in closed oligopolistic markets. This normally creates a business environment in which barriers to entry of new competitors are very high, and a relatively unstable equilibrium is maintained between firms and economic groups. The point is that while competition at the firm level is often inhibited by collusive agreements, rivalry among the groups that usually control these companies can be very intense as they jockey for control of new sectors, critical inputs (including capital), or distribution channels.

It is natural that in a government-controlled economy, the result of this competition among diversified conglomerates depends critically on the decisions of government officials. This tends to politicize the behavior of these conglomerates. Therefore, for many years in Venezuela, the main skills that the environment required businessmen and managers to hone had more to do with influencing politicians, civil servants, and journalists than with attracting consumers or persuading investors.

It was difficult to survive the threats of a constantly changing policy environment and the predatory moves of rivals without having access to politicians and policymakers and the means to influence them. Having close ties with union leaders who could oppose or promote a specific government decision in the name of the "working class" became a frequently utilized tactic. Another was to employ journalists as well-paid "consultants" who could write or broadcast well-targeted "news" about competitors or influence government decisions through the media. The profitability of a gain in productivity obtained by many years of hard work or significant investments could be completely wiped out by the connivance of a public regulator with a rival, or by its control of the main—and usually the only—local source of raw materials for the operation. It was therefore not uncommon for large groups to develop very sophisticated intelligence-gathering capacities that normally included the hiring of retired or even active police officers and intelligence professionals. A tape containing the private telephone gossip of a rival or a government official could be infinitely more profitable than the design specifications of a new product, for example.

With the added domestic and foreign competition brought about by market-oriented reforms and by deregulation, the delicate oligopolistic equilibrium that existing conglomerates may have achieved is lost. In certain cases this in turn pushes some of these large conglomerates into a competitive frenzy in which they make use of all the competitive weapons at their disposal, including, of course, government officials, politicians, journalists, union leaders, and "intelligence gatherers."

The deregulation of the financial sector or the stock market, the privatization of large public utilities, the takeover of existing firms in alliance with foreign investors, and countless other possibilities, open the door for new competition among business groups. Although their traditional politically based competitive weapons may in the long run lose much of their effectiveness and may even be abandoned in the transition, they continue to play a major role as tools to support the conglomerates' business strategies.

It is easy to imagine the added complexity, disinformation, and instability such behavior instills in an already turbulent and confusing political environment.

A Weak State and Weak Political Parties

Perhaps no other factor contributed as much to determine the political instability that followed the attempted coup as the weakness of the state.

The Venezuelan state has often been accused of being too rich, thanks to its oil revenues, or too big due to its ownership of a large array of firms of all kinds, or perhaps too powerful due to its control and intervention in most aspects of economic and even social life in the country. The paradox, however, is that having all those attributes has weakened it enormously in terms of the reliability of its institutions and its capacity to perform basic functions with a modicum of efficiency. The demands on the state were not only propelled by population growth and rising expectations. The policy approach that prevailed for three decades also added substantial pressures to increase the scope of the state's action. This ever-expanding scope constantly burdened the public sector with new functions and responsibilities. Furthermore, whereas the scope of the state's involvement constantly increased, its capacity to perform tended to decrease at an even faster pace. The chronic fiscal crisis of the Venezuelan state made it impossible to sustain funding levels appropriate to the expanded public functions. Furthermore, the organizational capacity to deliver was severely eroded by a civil service that was underpaid, undertrained, and plagued by turnover, corruption, congestion, and politicization.

The state was weakened not only by the *quantity* and variety of the policies that it had to formulate, implement, finance, and monitor—it was also weakened by the *quality* of the policies it had to implement, which normally relied on an inordinate amount of discretion by the bureaucracy. This propensity to empower a fragile bureaucracy with substantial discretion created an even more fertile ground for corruption to bloom. It provided great incentives for individuals and groups with particular interests to center all their efforts in forcing or persuading bureaucrats and politicians to make biased decisions and special concessions in their favor. This in turn greatly contributed to minimizing the state's capacity for independent action, thus further eroding its performance.

In fact, the logical consequence of this trend was that over time the state became more and more focused on responding to the pressures, needs, and requests of influential groups and individuals. This particularistic bias, in turn, naturally decreased its capacity to implement policies and make decisions aimed at serving the population as a whole. In this way the state, and in particular the executive branch, tended to rely for political support on the goodwill of specific groups which benefited from the situation, while neglecting the development of more general support that confers the true legitimacy on which autonomous state action ultimately rests.

The interesting paradox is that by choosing, in 1989, an economic policy aimed at transferring to the market many important decisions that had traditionally been within the purview of government officials, a very weak state deliberately became even weaker. Suddenly, the power to allocate foreign exchange, set prices, allow a specific product to be imported or banned, or assign or withhold a social subsidy, was surrendered to the private sector. Naturally this alienated the influential groups and individuals that offered their support to all recent governments in exchange for their privileged access to these special favors. Notable among these influential groups whose favor the government lost, was its own party—Acción Democrática—which, like all political parties in the country in recent years, had come to rely almost exclusively on its ability to act as a broker in the distribution of the state's favors. The government's surprising decision to reduce its discretion on economic matters left the party with very little to offer to its members, given that ideology and other such moral incentives had long ceased to be important as sources of partisan commitment.

This was not an exclusive problem of Acción Democrática. All political parties and institutions—including those representing labor, business, and professional guilds—suffered the consequences of having relied for too long on the special concessions they were able to extract from a rich and easily influenced state to justify their existence in practice. Furthermore, within all parties and political institutions a significant rift emerged between those which continued to be committed to the more statist and nationalistic model of import-substituting industrialization and the small but growing groups that favored a more market- and export-oriented approach.

These internal divisions, together with the deep ideological confusions brought about by the changes occurring in the world and in the country, and the extremely feeble institutional foundations and organizational capabilities of all political parties, greatly eroded their internal cohesiveness. It also limited their capacity to define and sustain a coherent political strategy, thus limiting their effectiveness as political actors.

The weakness of political parties and other organizations facilitated the launching of the reforms by limiting the effectiveness of the opposition to the government initiatives. The early failures of the factions opposed to the reforms to block their implementation, and the evident state of disarray within all political parties, convinced the government that a coalition with these other parties was neither possible nor, perhaps, indispensable.

The attempted coup changed all that. Although the lack of strong leadership and a unifying political strategy within the parties continued to limit their effectiveness in imposing a change of course on the government, the failed coup boosted the opposition and weakened the government. It also made it necessary for the government to try and broaden its political base. Unfortunately, the capacity of political parties to be effective members of a coalition government, increase popular support for the government or for the reforms, or provide the votes in Congress needed to pass the government-proposed political and economic program, remained almost nonexistent. In fact, the internal divisions within the parties, and the strong public reaction against the government, made it very difficult to assemble a stable coalition that could act as an effective anchor for the country's political system and allow the government to continue its program.

The Media

The mass media was another significant source and reservoir of the political instability that emerged as a consequence of the government's decision to relinquish its discretionary power over economic decisions. Like most other private firms in the country, newspapers, television, and radio networks were also part of diversified conglomerates with business interests in different sectors. As such, under the previous economic scheme they were critically dependent on the government's decisions for the success of the different businesses in which they were active. Freedom of expression had been a central tenet of democratic political life in the country. All governments were extremely sensitive to criticisms in this domain, and, in general, both the print and electronic media exhibited a quite adversarial attitude toward the government. Nonetheless, it was also very easy to discern that owners and editors had a clear albeit tacit understanding of the limits beyond which criticizing the government could become too costly.

Once this implicit inhibition was abandoned, mass media adopted an unprecedented vehemence in their attacks against the government, reporting and amplifying with a vengeance the most strident voices of the opposition.

Several forces pushed the media to adopt an extremely belligerent attitude against the Pérez administration: (1) Without a doubt, the general mood of the country was one of opposition to the government policies and of great anger toward the impunity of corrupt individuals. This was a social reality and therefore became an unavoidable element of any coverage of the country's news. The country was in a lynching mood and the demand for scapegoats was very high. The mood was also one of heightened competition between business firms, including the media, who competed fiercely to satisfy their clients' demands; (2) There is a normal propensity for the mass media in democratic societies to develop adversarial relationships with those in power; (3) Media conglomerates also engaged in the oligopolistic wars referred to above and were part and parcel of that process, with all its ensuing consequences; (4) In some cases, media owners continued to press the government for special concessions. If the government acquiesced, the oligopolistic rivals of those favored would retaliate against it. If, instead, the government would deny the special concession, those turned down would also retaliate. In all cases, some aspect of the government—not necessarily related to the specific demand—was bound to be severely criticized; (5)

For a variety of reasons, journalists tended to strongly oppose the economic reform program of the Pérez government. Their training made them very suspicious and distrustful of the market, and as a social group they were part of the socioeconomic stratum that was hardest hit by inflation and lower living standards. They also suffered as a professional group from the neglect in economic education that was prevalent in the country and therefore made it more difficult for them to understand and report with accuracy and clarity the nature, purposes, and consequences of the government's economic decisions. Journalists in the government also exhibited the same attitudes and limitations, thus restricting the government's ability to develop an effective information strategy that could at least partially offset the effects of the strong opposition by journalists and media owners.

The government exhibited a systematic incapacity to recognize that, under the circumstances, an effective communication strategy had to be one of its top priorities. Instead, a very weakened government continued to handle its public information policies with the same institutions and attitudes it had inherited. It systematically ignored the fact that under the new circumstances of its own making it now lacked some of the instruments on which it had relied in the past to limit the capacity of media owners and journalists to hold it hostage to their passions and interests. In the past, the possibility of using the subtle but powerful influence generated by the many economic decisions under its control made it possible for the government to neglect the development of a reliable capacity to inform the public and explain government decisions without the intermediation of interested parties. Such an institutional capacity would not have prevented the political turmoil that emerged. But it could certainly have contributed to reducing the tensions produced by the voicelessness of a government that was trying to introduce major societal changes.

The Political Management of Economic Change: What to Learn from the Venezuelan Turmoil

The political instability that rocked thirty-four years of uninterrupted democratic regimes in Venezuela was welcomed for its vindication of the domestic and international critics of the economic approach adopted by the Venezuelan government in 1989. Opposition leaders, social commentators, and academics in Venezuela and in countries where similar reform programs were being implemented saw in the Venezuelan political crisis the evidence needed to confirm the idea that such programs were a big mistake, if not outright folly. The crisis confirmed claims that market-oriented reforms inflict excessive burdens on the poor and middle classes and are therefore socially and politically intolerable; and it boosted demands for either the outright rejection and reversal of these policies or the imperative need to embrace gradualism and abandon shock therapies that risk killing the patient or causing irreversible collateral damage. After all, if Venezuela, a country with vast resources, a well-established democratic tradition, and a situation that had rapidly made it one of the darlings of international investors, could not implement these reforms with a minimum of social peace, what would be the effects—and the chances of success—for such policies in Nicaragua, Peru, Algeria, or the Philippines?

Should the "Shock Treatment" to Policy Reform Be Avoided?

As these pages have shown, the determinants of the Venezuelan crisis make it very difficult to establish a direct causality between the specific nature of the economic reforms undertaken and the strong political instability that emerged.

In 1989, Venezuela was on the verge of hyperinflation, confronting both a severe balance-of-payments crisis and a fiscal crisis. At the same time, drastic shortages of food, medicines, and raw materials were emerging everywhere, the country had lost its international creditworthiness, and the institutional capacity of the state to execute public policies was reduced to a minimum.

In fact, there are ample reasons to believe that in the nineties, regardless of the economic policy approach taken by the government, Venezuelans will experience the worst economic and social situation in the last three decades, together with the political instability that such a situation implies. Any government that came to power in 1989 would have had to bear the burden of being in charge of paying for the economic sins and mistakes of the past.

The government chose to address the macroeconomic problems with very drastic and swiftly implemented reforms. This shock therapy approach undoubtedly had a major destabilizing effect on the economy and on society. It also corrected major macroeconomic disequilibria in less than three years. These drastic economic measures were not determined by a stubborn government's ideological preference for painful shocks, whose avoidance only depended on political will to choose a more gradual pace of change. Instead, they were the consequence of the very practical impossibility to do otherwise.[17]

Many observers argue that alternative policies could have been implemented, but that the adoption of a shock treatment to policy reform in Venezuela was simply a consequence of it being a nonnegotiable condition of the International Monetary Fund and the World Bank. But a comparison of the agreements reached in 1989 with these institutions indicates that in some policy areas (notably price decontrol, the exchange rate regime, interest rate decontrol, and trade reform) the government had a significant margin of flexibility in terms of the pace needed to implement such policy changes. The main determinants of the government's own decision to move faster in these areas were its discovery that the existing institutions were incapable of administering a more gradualistic transition, that changing one policy exerted strong pressures for similarly paced change in another policy, or the government's conviction that a slower pace of reform would allow the opponents of the reforms to gain strength and be able to block them altogether.

It could even be argued that those decisions that were delayed, therefore injecting a dose of gradualism into the process, contributed significantly to political instability. Delays in congressional approval of reform in the tax system weakened the fiscal stance and made inflation more resilient. The strong political opposition to increased gasoline prices, together with the government's incompetence in designing a more efficient system to protect the poor from rate increases in public transportation, also created a gradualistic change that became a constant source of street demonstrations and political friction.

This, of course, does not mean that the government was faultless in designing and implementing the reform process. In fact, the Venezuelan experience highlights several important lessons about launching and managing radical large-scale policy changes. However, not many of the problems encountered by the government in the implementation of the reforms would have been avoided by reducing the pace of reform. Paradoxically, many of the problems originated in the government's sluggishness in instituting effective institutional reforms in certain areas.

The Urgency of Strengthening Public Institutions

Although macroeconomic stabilization and growth are important priorities, the weakness of public institutions should be addressed effectively from the beginning. This is a complex, time-consuming process, and resources are rarely available to undertake such changes effectively across the entire spectrum of public institutions. It should be realized, therefore, that it will be necessary to select a group of critical public institutions and focus on them. In this sense it is important to note that while one of the objectives of market reforms is to "get prices right," one of the prices that is often left to lag grossly behind is that of salaries paid to senior and middle managers in the public sector. This distortion adds to the weakness of a state that is introducing changes that, as we saw, are bound to weaken it even more. Although across-the-board salary increases in the public sector are not advisable until the fiscal stance is strengthened, it should be a priority to identify the institutions whose technical weaknesses and lack of a reliable pool of professional talent can jeopardize the entire reform program.

The implementation of grand plans to reform the state normally takes a long time and is bureaucratically and politically burdensome. These ambitious plans should not be allowed to interfere with the special attention that a select group of critical institutions requires very early in the reform process.

Macroeconomic Stabilization Without Running Water, Working Hospitals, and Public Transportation Does Not Buy Political Support

There is probably nothing more politically sensitive than to attempt an upgrade in the efficiency of agencies in charge of providing public services (water, sanitation, public transportation, and so forth) or delivering social services like health, education, or assistance to the poor. These organizations are normally the largest employers and therefore have very active unions closely connected with the political system. Furthermore, a strike in any of these agencies is bound to carry a heavy political cost and be a source of significant turmoil. Therefore, given the instability typically accompanying the initial stages of macroeconomic stabilization (devaluation, price increases, recession, and so forth), it is very natural to conclude that other decisions that are expected to cause even more social and political agitation should be postponed. The restructuring of the health or the education ministries, for example, is usually so politically threatening that it tends to be postponed until after the political waves caused by macroeconomic adjustment decisions subside.

Following the examples of other countries, in Venezuela, new social services delivery institutions were created to bypass existing agencies. Although the result was that new social programs were rapidly implemented, an added source of bureaucratic rivalry, inefficiency, and delays in responding to the critical needs of society was also created. Moreover, the new bypassing institutions and their programs created the illusion in the government that difficult decisions about the institutional decay of the main public agencies could be further postponed.

It would be very naive to attempt to prescribe precise guidelines on the dosage of politically sensitive measures a government should take or on the pacing of such reforms. But certain lessons should be kept in mind. First is that not much else can be effectively reformed if the country is in the grips of runaway inflation. Hence the importance of rapid macroeconomic stabilization. But also, as the Venezuelan case clearly illustrates, the negative political consequences of not having more efficient public services and social security agencies cannot be offset for very long by progress achieved on the macroeconomic front, regardless of how substantial that is.

Restructuring the Economy Requires the Adjustment
of the State's Public Information Policies

Nothing smooths over changes involving individuals, groups, and organizations like information and communication. The Venezuelan government systematically ignored this fact, and was oblivious to the need to approach this problem area with the same attention, resources, and preoccupation it devoted to the other changes it was introducing. Major reforms need to be explained systematically in very accessible and easily understandable terms. Very often, government officials in charge of implementing complex innovations in public policies lack skills and capacity to make their decisions intelligible to the general public. Add to this an adversarial media, a constant flow of new and largely unknown concepts, acronyms, and institutions, journalists who lack the training to adequately translate technical concepts into common language, and the distortions introduced by parties interested in confusing an issue, and the result is yet another major source of social confusion and political friction.

The important point is not only to develop an effective communication and information strategy, but also to create institutional arrangements to ensure that such a strategy can be implemented with precision over a long period of time. In many cases, existing institutions and approaches are inadequate, tending to be rooted in conditions that were prevalent when the state had a much greater influence over the media than it does now in the wake of economic deregulation of the communications sector.

These are just some of the lessons emphasized during the recent Venezuelan experience with economic change. The evolution of that country's situation will certainly provide many other lessons. But contrary to the assessment of many observers, the main determinant of future stability will not be the pace at which market-oriented reforms will be introduced. Instead, the defining element will have more to do with the capacity of the state to muster the resources—political, institutional, and human—to be more autonomous and effective in its decisions than it had ever been in the past.

The state will have to develop strength for modernizing and adapting the institutional framework and organizational structure of the armed forces. It will have to become an effective regulator of economic life and curb the political and commercial excesses of oligopolies accustomed to substantial influence in shaping government decisions. Similarly, it will have to restrain the influence of union bosses and their patrons in the political parties on the day-to-day operations of public agencies, especially those in the social sector. It will also have to confront the mafias that for many years have made a sad joke of the country's judicial system. These are not tasks for a weak state. Neither is reforming society.

Appendix 1
Leaflet Distributed in the Streets of Caracas[18]
(February–March 1992)

To the Venezuelan People

The Bolivarian Military Movement, seeks, through this document, to challenge the smear campaign which has been launched against us, the Bolivarian Military, represented by our Commander Hugo Chávez Frías. In this regard, we hereby declare that:

First: The main objective of our Movement is the recovery of the Bolivarian ideal in all its expressions, and the dignity of being a soldier to serve the interests of the Venezuelan nation.

Second: To establish an emergency government comprised of the most honorable people of our country, to recover the values of the Venezuelan citizenry and to eliminate the rampant corruption of the past 34 years engendered by those who, without moral or social justification, label us as criminals.

Third: To confiscate all the assets of the politicians who have enriched themselves by plundering the national treasury and money from international loans. All these confiscated resources will be used to pay the external debt.

Fourth: To prepare the indictments for those accused of corruption and high treason to our country, in order to initiate the corresponding judicial procedures in accordance with the Constitution and the laws of the Republic, ensuring them that their individual rights, as they are established according to the rule of law, will be observed. All of this would take place under the supervision of representatives of the Interamerican Court of Human Rights.

Under no circumstances do we intend to establish a dictatorship or to curtail constitutional rights, nor to violate any human rights. The only democracy which was endangered was the one associated with CAP, Ciliberto, Lusinchi, Blanca Ibañez, Vinicio Carrera, RECADI, Porfirio

173

Valera, Avila Vivas, Henry López Sisco, Antonio Ríos, David Morales Bello, Luis Herrera, Eduardo Fernández and Teodoro Petkoff, among others.[19]

We would also like to express our condemnation of the owners of the media who, acting with complicity, misrepresented the feelings of the Venezuelan people regarding the events of February 4.

Finally, we want to make clear that our Commander Hugo Chávez Frías, as well as all the members of our movement, have a Bolivarian ideal. Therefore, he will never attempt to take his own life, and his physical elimination would only be possible by the criminal and corrupted hands of those who still flaunt their power.

We are committed and we will never renounce our commitment and our oath to the country and to the Bolivarian way of thinking, which is why we have made an effort to be an elite battalion with an impeccable record.

WE DID NOT LOSE THE WAR, BUT ONLY ONE BATTLE AMONG MANY OTHERS STILL NEEDED TO ACHIEVE BOLIVAR'S PATRIA!

WE STILL HAVE A LOT OF CHÁVEZES!

THE CRIMINALS ARE IN THE GOVERNMENT AND IN CONGRESS!

LONG LIVE OUR COMMANDER CHÁVEZ AND OUR HEROIC BATTALION OF RED BERETS!

The Bolivarian Civil-Military Movement

Appendix 2
Leaflet Distributed in the Streets of Caracas[20]
(February–March 1992)

For Now

On the fourth of February, the people woke up full of hopes for the insurrection by an important sector of progressive soldiers and civilians opposed to 34 years of democratic farce. Not knowing for certain the intentions of the rebels, we all quickly began to identify with the movement. We identified because we are fed up with so much misery, with so many lies, with so few people benefiting from the immense wealth of our country. But the expressions of happiness which began to appear in the faces of working people were frustrated *"for now."* Nevertheless, the inexhaustible support of the people for the civilian and military insurgency has revealed the possibility of a radical change in favor of the great majority of the people. The opportunity to be "free of the obstacles imposed by bureaucracy, party rule and corruption" is in our hands . . . We shall return!!!

FOR THE RESCUE OF BOLÍVAR'S HOMELAND!

NEXT TIME ALL OF US TO MIRAFLORES . . . !!! DOWN WITH THE FORCES LOYAL TO CORRUPTION!

Notes

The author was the minister of Industry of Venezuela during the initial two years of the reform process discussed here, and is currently an executive director of the World Bank in Washington, D.C. All the information and data contained in the following pages comes from publicly available sources. The findings, interpretations, and conclusions expressed here are entirely those of the author and should not be attributed in any manner to the governments he represents or to the World Bank. Thanks are due to Alan Batkin, Robert Bottomme, Jonathan Coles, Judith Evans, Larry Fabian, Peter Hakim, Abraham Lowenthal, Francisco Sagasti, Strobe Talbott, Gustavo Tarre, Gerver Torres, and Joseph S. Tulchin for their comments on an earlier draft of this chapter, reprinted here with the permission of the Carnegie Endowment for International Peace.

1. In its August 1991 report, the International Country Risk Guide rated Venezuela the least risky country in Latin America and the twenty-fifth best investment site among 129 countries worldwide. Venezuela ranked higher than South Korea, Spain, Thailand, and Hong Kong, among others. *Euromoney* magazine, in its September 1991 issue, increased Venezuela's ranking from sixty-fourth place in 1990 to forty-fifth in 1991, according to its analytical, credit, and market indicators. Standard and Poor's *Credit Week International* (August 5, 1991) upgraded Venezuela's Eurobond rating from BB to BB plus, while Moody's Bond Survey (August 1991) also increased the quality of its bonds from Ba3 to Ba1. (See CONAPRI, 1991, "Venezuela Update" (Caracas: National Council for Investment Promotion).)

2. One of the most peculiar aspects of the coup was that the rebels did not seem to give much priority to gaining control over radio and TV stations, or public utilities like power and telephone service. In fact, rebel soldiers went to one of the private television stations only to discover that while its studios were still there, its broadcasting facilities had been moved to another location more than three years earlier. Another group of soldiers took over the public television station and requested to broadcast a message to the nation, a message that had been taped by their leaders and which they had brought in a videocassette. The president of the station convinced the officer in charge of the group that the format of their videotape was incompatible with the station's, and that it was going to take a while to arrange for its conversion to the format suited for broadcast. This subterfuge stalled the process long enough for loyal forces to gain control of the situation. The broadcast of the rebels' taped message

obviously would have undermined the effect of the fact that the only public announcements to the population during the events were those of the president and his supporters denouncing the coup and announcing that the government was rapidly gaining control of the situation. Events would have unfolded in a very different way had the rebels gained operational control of at least some radio and TV stations.

3. General Fernando Ochoa Antich, the minister of Defense, has acknowledged that allowing Chávez to go live on television was a major mistake caused by the confusion surrounding the process, his impatience to get all the rebels that were still resisting to surrender as soon as possible, and the fact that by that time he had gone without sleep for more than 48 hours.

4. Caldera's move was in line both with his permanent disagreement with the market-oriented policies, and with his wishes to be reelected in the 1993 presidential election. He maintained a very bitter dispute with Eduardo Fernández, his onetime protége, and since the previous election, his successful contender for COPEI's presidential nomination. Fernández enjoyed wide support within the party, having for all practical purposes firm control over it, thus ensuring his nomination and probably his presidential election. Since the end of the 1988 campaign, Caldera had been actively working to erode and minimize Fernández's presidential chances. Caldera took a radical and systematic public stance against the market approach to economic policies that Pérez and Fernández supported, and was in the process of bringing together a coalition of leftist parties, independents, and the remainder of his supporters within COPEI to seek election in 1993, or at least to impede Fernández's electoral success.

5. Lieutenant Colonels Hugo Chávez, Francisco J. Arias, Manuel Urdaneta, and José Ortiz.

6. Appendix 1 presents a translation of a leaflet that was widely distributed in the streets of Caracas a few days after the coup claiming to be an official statement of the "Bolivarian Military Movement" and "our Commander Hugo Chávez" in which a summary of the group's ideas and goals is presented. Appendix 2 presents a translation of another flyer distributed in Caracas after the coup.

7. The night of the coup, loyal officers who had surrounded Chávez and his troops established telephone contact with him to request that he surrender. Although accepting his military defeat, he repeatedly told them that he had to wait until morning for the people to find out what was happening and take to the streets to rally against the government and rise in support of the rebels. The popular support that the rebels had assumed never materialized during the coup. Many other details about their assumptions and tactics and the fact that they did not seem to have had any contingency plan if their goal of capturing or killing the president failed, seem to point towards a very unsophisticated and rather primitive approach on the part of the plotters.

8. Less than one hundred officers and around nine hundred soldiers were arrested and brought before military tribunals.

9. On the institutional front, the president sent to Congress a bill overhauling the judicial system. The proposal would streamline procedures, remove incompetent or corrupt judges, and prohibit judges from being members of political parties. He also announced the intensification of the campaign against corruption and announced new procedures for extraditing individuals from abroad who were accused of corruption. Furthermore, he requested that Congress approve his proposal to reduce the number of ministries from twenty-six to nine in order to cut down on bureaucracy.

Among the social measures, he stated that housing subsidies directed at the poor would be extended to the middle class in general, and army officers in particular. He also indicated that the social security system would be restructured and that a massive program of public transportation would be initiated, as would a major expansion of a university scholarship program.

On economic matters, Pérez announced that the program to gradually increase the price of gasoline would be suspended as would—temporarily—the scheduled increases in the price of electricity, and that the prices of five food staples would be stabilized by the government. New taxes, levied on the acquisition of luxury goods and corporate assets, were also going to be proposed to Congress, as well as new laws to make tax evasion a criminal offense, and to modernize and strengthen the supervision of commercial banks and the stock market. Finally, the president announced that a referendum to initiate the process of constitutional reform was going to be held in the following months, and that he was going to form a new cabinet of "national unity" with the participation of members of other political parties. A telling anecdote is that only one of these announcements made the live audience comprised of congressmen of all political parties stand up and applaud and was headlined by all major newspapers the next day: the suspension of the planned increases in gasoline prices. In Venezuela low prices for gasoline have very regressive consequences in terms of income distribution, given the pattern of consumption among different socioeconomic groups and the consequences of low gas prices on government revenue. These consequences on public revenue weaken the state's fiscal stance, thus fueling inflation which, as we know, is a highly regressive economic phenomenon in terms of income distribution. Since the beginning, the government was completely unsuccessful in explaining this to the public, instead allowing gasoline prices to acquire a symbolic value that made them a focal point for the opposition to the reform program (see Chapter 4 in this volume).

Of all the proposals sketched by Pérez in his speech, only those that could be implemented autonomously by the administration were actually implemented.

10. Pérez replaced the resigning foreign minister with General Fernando Ochoa Antich, the minister of Defense, appointing in his place another general—Ivan Dario Jiménez—known for his commitment to democracy and his strong attachment to established institutional rules. This move helped dissipate the tensions within the armed forces that traditionally emerge every year in the months preceding the replacement of the minister of Defense as the incumbent minister maneuvers to stay on and other aspiring high-ranking officials also maneuver to be appointed. Such a complex process in the midst of the ongoing instability was bound to be more turbulent than normal. Pérez preempted this possibility with his decision.

11. The most extreme example of the utilization of such tactics seemed to have happened one night in late 1987, when a group of tanks surrounded the presidential palace and soldiers took control of the offices of the ministry of the Interior. At the time, the president, Jaime Lusinchi, was out of the country on a state visit and the minister of the Interior, Simon Alberto Consalvi, was the acting president. Consalvi was in his office when an officer entered to inform him that he had been sent, together with the tanks, to protect him. The surprised acting president called the minister of Defense at home, only to discover that the minister was as surprised as he was and ordered the officer to return with the tanks to their barracks, which they did. The ensuing inquiry showed that the incident was initiated by a call to the commander of the tank unit by a person who, after identifying himself as a senior officer and utilizing the correct secret

codes, ordered the tank commander to take his unit to the presidential palace to defend the acting president from an imminent attack. The investigation concluded that the call could not have been made by the officer under whose name the instruction had been given and that the tank commander had been tricked by the bogus order. Although some have interpreted this incident as a failed coup that was just a preview of the events of 1992, others are convinced that its main purpose was to embarrass and discredit the army generals responsible for that unit and thus torpedo their promotion.

12. World Bank (1992), *Global Economic Prospects and the Developing Countries, March.*

13. Employment data is from the national household survey (Encuesta de Hogares) while macroeconomic data are from METROECONÓMICA (1991, 1992), *Hechos y Tendencias de le Economia Venezolana* (Caracas: Monthly Economic Bulletin, several issues).

14. The sources of these statistics are the private sector industry associations, FENAVI, CAVIDEA, CAVEDIV, CAVENEZ, FADAM, METROECONÓMICA's February, 1992 report, the Venezuelan-American Chamber of Commerce's economic report, and DATOS (National Store Audit, 1991).

15. Márquez, Gustavo (1992), "Poverty and Social Policies in Venezuela." Paper presented at the Brookings Institution and Inter-American Dialogue's Conference, "Poverty and Inequality in Latin America" (Washington, D.C.: July 1992).

16. Naím, M. (1992), "The Launching of Radical Policy Changes: The Venezuelan Experience." Chapter 4 in this volume.

17. For a more detailed discussion of this point, see Chapter 4 in this volume.

18. Translated by Manuela de Rangel and Martin Van Opdorp.

19. CAP are the initials of President Pérez; Lusinchi and Herrera Campins are former presidents. Carrera and Ciliberto were cabinet members in previous administrations and, after having been charged with corruption, fled the country. Ibañez was President Lusinchi's private secretary and is now his wife. She, too, lives abroad after having been indicted by the Venezuelan courts. Valera and Lopez Sisco are former high-ranking members of DISIP, the state security police. Ríos was the president of CTV, the Workers Federation, and had to step down under pressure after having been accused of corruption. Avila Vivas was governor of the Federal District (Caracas), Morales Bello was president of Congress, Fernández is the secretary-general of the Christian Democratic party—COPEI— and Petkoff is a former guerrilla commander who has been one of the founding leaders of Movimiento al Socialismo—MAS—the third most important party in Venezuela.

20. Translated by Manuela de Rangel and Martin Van Opdorp.

Index

Abente, Diego, 17, 137
Acción Democrática, 2, 5, 9, 45, 120, 122, 133; loss of congressional majority (1988), 47
AD party. *See* Acción Democrática
Agriculture, 40; and Pérez reforms, 8

Beca Alimentaria, 55-56
Betancourt, Rómulo, 2
Blanco, Antonio Guzmán, 25, 26
Blanco, Carlos, 16, 97
Bolivia; foreign investment, 51
Briceño, Gustavo Tarre, 17, 125
Budget deficit, 49-50

Caldera, Rafael, 2, 3, 126, 150-151, 177-178n.
Campins, Luis Herrera, 4, 44
Capital flight, 5, 78-79
Carré de Malberg, Raymond, 126
Central Bank, 61-62, 73, 91n.
Centralization; and democracy, 29-30; and oil, 29. *See also* Decentralization
Chávez Frías, Hugo, 11, 149-150
Chile; economic development, 112
Civil unrest; following Pérez election, 47-48, 88-90n., 91n., 120; resulting from economic adjustments, 7-8, 57
Conciencia, 34, 110
Consalvi, Simon Alberto, 179
COPEI, 2, 133, 154, 155; current attitude toward Pérez reforms, 120; and economic reform, 12; and German Christian Democrat model, 12; in election against Pérez, 119, 127; role in reforms, 17
COPRE, 16, 106; and democratization, 34
Corruption, 130, 161-163

Costa Rica; infant mortality rate, 52
Coup attempt (1992), 11, 18, 148; after-effects of, 151-156; arrests from, 178n.; and corruption, 161-163; detailed account of, 148-151; economic pressures contributing to, 158-161; leaders, 151-152, 178n.; leaflets distributed after, 174-176; lessons of, 168-173; and media, 167-168; media failure of rebels, 177n.; military changes contributing to, 156-158; mistaken assumptions of leaders, 178n.; and oligopolies, 163-164; reasons for failure of, 152; and weakness of state, 164-167. *See also* Opposition
Crime; following economic adjustments, 57
CTV, 149
Currency stability, 61-62
CVF. *See* Venezuelan Development Corporation

Damas, Germán Carrera, 15, 21
Decentralization, 34, 103, 121-122, 127-128. *See also* Centralization
Democracy; and centralization, 29-30; and communication, 35; and competition, 34; and decentralization, 34; dimensions of, 34-36; Freedom House ratings, 34-35; and law, 103; and poverty, 98-99; and republic, 141-142; role of opposition, 125; in United States, 35
Democratic development, 11, 15, 16, 17; abandonment of authoritarianism, 124; and economic reform, 33-34; effect on economic development, 97-98; first stage, 21-

About the Book

Venezuela, Latin America's second-oldest democracy, today faces its greatest challenge. Recovering from two military coups in 1992 and seeking resolution of a severe crisis of presidential legitimacy, the Pérez government must now fight for its survival.

This timely book explores the roots of Venezuela's current crisis. The authors trace the country's democratic development, offer in-depth studies of the processes of state reform and economic restructuring—the "Great Turnaround"—launched by President Pérez in 1989, discuss recent changes in Venezuela's foreign policy, and consider the role of the main political opposition. They also evaluate the first year of the Pérez government. Concluding with an insightful analysis of the startling events of February 4, 1992, and the institutional obstacles that Venezuela must now overcome, the book provides an excellent overview of the country at this critical juncture in its history.